Praise for *Sovereign Love*

"Dené Logan is a pioneering force in the landscape of couples work. *Sovereign Love* asks urgent and necessary questions that bravely shake the foundation of modern love—and offers readers the tools to rebuild the foundation anew."

ESTHER PEREL

psychotherapist, author, and host of *Where Should We Begin?*

"Wise and soulful, Dené Logan is shining a Technicolor flashlight on how our relationships can unwittingly suffocate our life force. This book is both a treatise and a treasure, giving people permission and a map toward claiming one's own unique path."

CHIP CONLEY

New York Times bestselling author and hospitality entrepreneur

"Dené Logan is a guiding light amid the messiness and murkiness of modern-day partnerships. Her wisdom goes beyond the traditional couples therapy model, challenging our conventional notions of love and belonging. She invites us not just into a journey of self-discovery and empowerment but also into a complete reimagining of what is possible in our connections when we show up as our full selves."

JEREMIE LOTEMO

poet and transformation coach

"Dené has a beautiful way of exploring how we approach love and relationships, helping us identify blind spots to bridging deeper and more meaningful connection. A beautiful must-read for everyone."

YASMINE CHEYENNE

author of *The Sugar Jar*

"Dené Logan's *Sovereign Love* is simply phenomenal. This is an exploration of the complexities of human connections. Her approach transcends traditional relationship paradigms, inviting readers into a transformative journey of self-awareness and mutual understanding. This book is not just a guide; it's a revelation that redefines the art of love and companionship in today's world, offering a vibrant blueprint for relating."

RAINIER WYLDE
teacher and author of *As You Are* and *Love Against Time*

SOVEREIGN
LOVE

SOVEREIGN LOVE

A GUIDE TO HEALING RELATIONSHIPS
BY RECLAIMING THE MASCULINE
AND FEMININE WITHIN

DENÉ LOGAN

MFT

sounds true
BOULDER, COLORADO

Sounds True
Boulder, CO

Published 2024

Cover design by Huma Akhtar
Book design by Meredith Jarrett

Printed in the United States of America

BK06862

Library of Congress Cataloging-in-Publication Data

Names: Logan, Dené, author.
Title: Sovereign love : a guide to healing relationships by reclaiming the masculine
    and feminine within / Dené Logan, AMFT.
Description: Boulder, CO : Sounds True, 2024. | Includes bibliographical
    references.
Identifiers: LCCN 2023037953 (print) | LCCN 2023037954 (ebook) | ISBN
    9781649632234 (trade paperback) | ISBN 9781649632241 (ebook)
Subjects: LCSH: Love. | Couples. | Man-woman relationships. |
    Interpersonal relations.
Classification: LCC BF575.L8 L65 2024 (print) | LCC BF575.L8
    (ebook) | DDC 152.4/1--dc23/eng/20231218
LC record available at https://lccn.loc.gov/2023037953
LC ebook record available at https://lccn.loc.gov/2023037954

FSC
www.fsc.org
MIX
Paper | Supporting
responsible forestry
FSC® C103098

for Darren

if you need permission to go,
I liberate you . . .
you see, love liberates.
it doesn't bind.
love says, "I love you.
I love you if you're in China,
I love you if you're across town,
I love you if you're in Harlem.
I love you.
I would like to be near you,
I'd like to have your arms around me,
I'd like to hear your voice in my ear.
but that's not possible now,
so—I love you. go."

Maya Angelou

Contents

Introduction:
My Fascination with Love . . .

"look inward—the loving begins with you."

OPRAH WINFREY

for most of my life, I was a love agnostic. I believed in love in theory —I have always loved rom-coms, and can't watch *The Notebook* without feeling a deep, subtle ache in the pit of my stomach. I love stories of people who've fought for their love through distance, and decades, and against everything logic would suggest made sense. But I just didn't really believe that that type of love was possible in real life—or at least not in a sustainable way.

Despite this personal ambivalence towards the concept of deep, abiding love, as I came into my private therapy practice, I found that I had a strange affinity for working with couples. I discovered that I could feel into the unspoken emotions that were happening beneath the surface for each person and subsequently playing out in their relationship dynamic, and I had an ability to interpret what I was seeing in a way that really shifted each person's perspective. As time went on, my work with these couples made me start to think that maybe I did believe in the possibility of a love that catalyzes deeper healing, supports our growth, and makes us feel seen. I began to think that maybe this type of love did exist for some people—and that I just hadn't experienced it personally.

You see, I was married for eleven and a half years. And although I was married to an incredible person who remains one of my best friends to this day, something about our union always felt a little bit off for me. After the expiration of my marriage, I began to view my work with couples through a different lens. I felt like a full-on relationship anthropologist. I had a unique perspective as a therapist, with firsthand knowledge of the variables that make long-term partnership so difficult. But with a little bit of distance from my own fears around my marriage coming to an end, I was able to view partnership with an objectivity I hadn't previously had.

With this newfound objectivity, I was able to notice a few important things. There are certain unspoken dynamics that I heard people grappling with so often, they began to seem like the inevitable realities of modern love and relationships. Here's a sampling of them:

- Women operating from a persistent baseline of anger and resentment about the share of the emotional labor they're carrying, feeling a general malaise and sense of burnout with their entire lives, and describing a feeling of exhaustion that no amount of rest can satiate.

- Couples living in such a deep state of enmeshment, that there's no sense of where one person begins, and the other person ends. This is a common occurrence in partnerships where each person feels like they've lost a sense of being an autonomous individual.

- Women consistently asking the men in their lives to be more open about how they're feeling yet becoming irritated the moment their partner attempts to use them as an emotional sounding board.

- One partner feeling frustrated with the lack of physical intimacy in the relationship, while the other person feels aggravated by what they consider to be a constant squabble about sex.

- The survival strategies developed by couples in childhood creating a dance of pulling love in, but then pushing it away once it gets close. This dynamic makes it nearly impossible for many people to experience emotional intimacy—both while dating and once in a committed partnership.

- An overall sense of dissatisfaction with the reality of what the quest for romantic love and partnership in modern times has turned out to be. The responsibilities, lack of aliveness, and constant bickering make partnership a vast departure from the fulfillment we're conditioned to believe we'll experience once we find "the one."

What's been interesting about witnessing these dynamics unfold for my clients is that they are the same variables I experienced in my own eleven-and-a-half-year marriage. I too experienced the feeling of needing something more from a partnership but being unable to crack the code of how to feel relational fulfillment. While attempting to connect the dots of my own experience of marriage and divorce with the patterns I observed with my clients, I've come to understand that there are internal dynamics that are rarely discussed in mainstream conversations about romantic love and relationships: most specifically, the interplay of the masculine and feminine energy everyone inherently possesses.

Swiss psychiatrist and founder of analytical psychiatry Carl Jung was the first to point out in his work that the human psyche is made up of elements that could be considered both "masculine" and "feminine" ways of being. And while both masculine and feminine polarities are present in every person and every relationship, when we are unaware of the interplay of these dynamics within ourselves and those around us, I have found that it creates an internal struggle as well as a sense of disharmony with any partner we choose.

Once I made this discovery and explored it deeper, I began to see it from a cultural and historical perspective:

- A wounded patriarchal culture has caused women to pass down internalized contempt for their internal feminine through the generations, creating conflict within and resentment towards their partners.

- A patriarchal society has taught men that the only acceptable outlets for feeling their emotions are through anger and sex, cultivating a culture where men are incapable of experiencing intimacy in their romantic partnerships.

Carrying these wounds has created a sense of disintegration in our partnerships.

My practice has shifted towards integrating these polarities—first within ourselves, and then within our relationships. To me, understanding these dynamics is the key to ending the unspoken war of the sexes that I see playing out every day in our relationships. I have found that an increased awareness of these dynamics helps the couples I work with move away from codependent, transactional views of what relationships "should" be, towards an interdependent, harmonious state where both partners are present, self-aware, and strong in Self.

This book walks you through the process of reclaiming the (capital S) Self and understanding how the integration of our inner masculine and feminine is the path to finding a sense of peace within, as well as the key to experiencing fulfillment in all of our relationships. In combining my personal revelations as a therapist with a modernized conversation around what it means to love one another well and a feminist perspective on resisting patriarchal trappings, I hope to offer you a deep and yet tangible guide to greater self-awareness of what has shaped us, and how we can take responsibility for finding greater harmony in all of our relationship dynamics.

In order to share how I've come to this understanding, I realized I'd need to share some intimate details of my own story. While there are elements of my story that still feel extremely vulnerable for me to share, I often remind myself of something my friend John Kim wrote in his book, *Single on Purpose*: "Be courageous: when others relate to your story, your story becomes bigger than you."[1] So I'll be sharing an honest account of my own faltering journey of attempting to understand these concepts in my personal life, while also illustrating the methods I've used to support couples, providing tangible tools for working with masculine and feminine energetics, and practicing interdependence within our partnerships moving forward.

Unfortunately, integrating these ideas is not as simple as taking a quick love language quiz or watching a masculine vs. feminine video on TikTok (though those are fun and can be quite helpful). This is work that requires a deep dive into our internal landscape to unpack the historical, cultural, and highly individual reasons of why we love the way we do. Once we understand our motivations, we can choose to consciously love in a way that serves us and acts as a catalyst for growth. I've seen the incredible impact this shift has had on my own relationships as well as the couples I've worked with, and I feel called to share these revelations and techniques with you in the hopes of supporting others in experiencing the wholehearted, satiating kind of love that is rooted in self-awareness and interdependence.

I've split the book into three parts to help guide you on the path to understanding the interplay of these dynamics. The significance of these three parts is based on the human process of **individuation**, as defined by Carl Jung. Jung suggested that in the first half of our life (normally up until about thirty years old), we are oriented toward the external world, which is typically associated with a more masculine energy. We are conditioned to believe that we will be safe if we follow a specific formula for what it means to live a good life: go to school, get a good job, get married, etc. As we begin to shift toward midlife, there is normally a catalyzing event that causes us to begin the **individuation process,** prompting us to look within (an activity which is associated with feminine energy) and question the sense of certainty we carried up to this point. This event can be a divorce, death of a loved one, or some other significant loss of identity. Finally, after we go on our own personal hero's journey into our inner world to identify a sense of truth within our own experience, we return to our villages, so to speak, forever changed. This part of the process represents an integration of our masculine and feminine energetics and brings a new sense of awareness about how we want to live—and ultimately, how we want to love.

The collective misunderstanding of our need to move through an individuation process is, from my perspective, so much of what has been missing from our psychological explorations of love and relationships, and also what has been causing such deep discord in our partnerships. This is a vital stage of human development that our society has completely lost its connection to. The integration of our own masculine and feminine energetics (which is essentially our ability to stay grounded in a solid sense of Self, while knowing that we will continue to evolve and change) is the third stage of our individuation process.

I've broken down the understanding of these three stages throughout the book as follows:

Stage One: STRUCTURE

- experiencing the world through the lens of a **masculine energetic**

- oriented toward the external

- complete identification with physical form (ego)

- rules of life have been laid out by an external authority

Stage Two: SEEKING

- shifting our experience of the world toward a **feminine energetic**

- orientation begins to shift toward the internal

- longing to feel connected to something larger (Soul)

- questioning of what might be true beyond what we've been conditioned to believe

Stage Three: SOVEREIGN

- tangible integration of masculine and feminine energetics

- emphasis on defining self and relationships from an embodied sense of Truth

- longing to be of service in relationships from a space of love instead of fear

- seeing relationships as an ever-evolving curriculum, helping us to expand and find deeper layers of healing

Throughout the exploration of these stages, I'll help you identify your core energetic, what energetic you've been operating from and why, the polarities between masculine and feminine that are being created in your partnerships, and how to take personal responsibility for shifting your own energy to a more integrated place. The identification of these energetic polarities has completely shifted everything I've come to understand about love. This is the work of understanding the practice of loving as a spiritual individuation process with the potential to bring us into deeper alignment with the Truth of who we are. It is the understanding that at its core, attempting to love another person is a process of healing.

My experiences on my own path to understanding these energetics ultimately broke my heart wide open in the best possible way, making me want to be a different kind of woman. I experienced everything I needed to in order to understand how we might find a sense of fulfillment in the most significant love affair we will have in this lifetime—the one with ourselves. This is that story. Not a single breath up to this point was wasted.

And so here is my hope and my prayer: to anyone who recognizes yourself in some aspect of what I've written in these pages, may this book serve as a guide to bring you back home to your (capital S) Self . . . so that when and if you decide to partner with another, you're bringing an authentic sense of Self to the union.

Stage One

STRUCTURE

CHAPTER 1

The Goal Is to Be Chosen

"if the path before you is clear, you're
probably on someone else's path."

JOSEPH CAMPBELL

Every Little Girl Dreams of Her Wedding Day, Right?

my wedding day was absolutely perfect. I got married in an outdoor ceremony in a little Canadian town near Niagara Falls called Niagara-on-the-Lake. The fact that it was such a beautiful day felt even more significant because of the amount of stress the torrential downpour the previous day had caused for all parties involved. But on the actual day of the wedding, it was like the Gods smiled down on us and determined that everything would be perfect. The white and pink flowers on the trees surrounding the aisle seemed to come into full bloom that morning, which coordinated perfectly with the pink peonies that had been chosen as the signature flower of the ceremony. The tuxedos and dresses, the table centerpieces and music choices, the perfect flower girl and ring bearer, lovely vows and pre-dinner toasts. Everything was picture perfect. It was somebody's dream come true. Just not mine.

I woke up early that morning. To say I was not feeling overwhelmed with pre-wedding jitters is certainly an understatement, because I spent most of the morning attempting to prevent the smell of marijuana from exiting my hotel room by stuffing towels underneath the cracks of the door while I got high with one of my best friends, and rustling through my luggage to search for the stash I'd wrapped in random dryer sheets and clothing to sneak my weed across the border. I was a wake-and-bake stoner at that point, and unbeknownst to everyone other than the friend I was spending the morning with, I'd been "stoned to bejeezus" every moment since I picked up my rental car when I arrived in Canada.

I'd made up some sort of bogus excuse for why I needed to travel separately so that my fiancé wouldn't interfere with my ability to anesthetize my way through this unbelievably joyous time. Although in all honesty—I think we both knew I had brought weed with me. We were continuing our already solidified practice of keeping secrets, sweeping things under the rug, and minimizing what felt a little too confrontational for us to talk about. He had, however, made one request of me for the day of our wedding: Please don't smoke pot on the actual day. I, of course, promised him I wouldn't. I, of course, smoked pot from the moment I woke up that morning, to the moment I passed out without consummating a damn thing that night.

I do, however, remember feeling a surge of overwhelming emotion for the first time that day as I made my way toward the aisle. My big brother was standing at the end of the aisle waiting to take me by the arm, and I could see tears begin to well in his eyes as he saw me. I don't think his tears had anything to do with seeing me all decked out in my wedding garb like a paper doll. I think they were more about the fact that weddings are one of the few ceremonial rites of passage that our culture has left. His little sister was being initiated into a new role in that moment. She was becoming someone's wife.

As we began our stroll down the flower-laden grassy aisle, I imagine that most people assumed my energy was focused on the extremely handsome groom who was patiently waiting to devote his entire life to me. It was not. All of my energy was focused on my mother. Was she happy? Did it all look the way she wanted it to look? Was this everything she'd been dreaming of for me? I just wanted her to approve.

I often tell people that I don't believe in regrets. And I truly don't. I think every aspect of our journey—even the cringe-worthy moments—has taught us something we needed to understand. And I hold my younger self with so much compassion when I think about how disconnected she was from any sense of self. She didn't know she had an alternative at the time, except to do what was expected of her. She was really just sleep-walking through her young life at that point—too afraid to wake up and take responsibility for who she wanted to be.

How Did We Get Here?

In grad school I studied depth psychology, which is often referred to as the psychology of the Soul. It explores the realms of our collective unconscious, including myths, archetypes, dreams, philosophy, and the shadow elements of our human experience. Studying depth psychology has taught me to prioritize curiosity as a first response to any given situation.

Because I now tend to view all of life through a bit of a depth psychology lens, I've given a lot of thought as to how I came to be that young woman I just described, who was so deeply disconnected from herself. What I've come to understand is that this level of self-abandonment is not at all unique to my experience. It's actually quite a societal norm. Our tendency to self-abandon has to do with the societal pressures placed upon us, the fear of exile that we instinctively know we will face if we choose to walk a different path from the one that's been laid out for us, and our earliest conditionings around creating safe and healthy attachments with our caregivers. In the midst of my quest for understanding the origins of my own self-abandonment, I started to notice these self-abandonment behavior patterns in others—and as a result, I began to envision a method for course correction. A path back to the reclamation of our Self, if you will.

At one point, I identified as an addict. I have since come to believe that we are all addicts to varying degrees, and that all our addictive tendencies are essentially maladaptive tools we use as an attempt to regulate our nervous systems. Meaning, when we are living out of alignment with the most fundamental truths of who we are, we develop unconscious coping strategies to manage the stress that living out of alignment places on our psyche. These coping strategies materialize in various forms of addictions: drugs and alcohol, gambling, shopping, sex, food, workaholism, and what is (to me) the most societally accepted addiction of them all—codependency.

Codependency is essentially a way that we learn to regulate our nervous system through our relationships to other people. We learn in our early attachment experiences to make ourselves feel safe by attempting to control our external environment—or other people. This can look like people pleasing, over-functioning for those around us, only showing others the aspects of ourselves that we believe they can tolerate seeing, and a host of other ways we learn to self-abandon early on.

According to the premise of Dr. Gabor Maté, a renowned addiction expert known for his expertise on trauma, addiction, stress, and childhood development, when a child is born they have two fundamental needs—the need for attachment (the experience of love and connection from our caretakers) and authenticity (an awareness of who we are and what we feel). But the need for attachment is a survival need, so it will always trump the need for authenticity. And because each of us has an instinctual need to form a healthy attachment to our caregivers, if that attachment feels contingent on us being compliant with our caretaker's desires, we will usually comply. And in doing so, we begin formulating the first blueprints of what will later be the origin of our codependent tendencies.[1]

To add another layer, as a woman, there are so many implicit messages we receive about who we are meant to be—long before we have the capacity to question the origin of these messages, or even if the values the messaging represents ring true to what we believe at our core. From the messaging in the Disney movies we grew up with, to watching our mothers attempting to maneuver through what it means to be a woman in this world, to the way we experience ourselves being met or rejected by our peers. A woman is expected to be impressive, productive, and intelligent—but not to the point where she intimidates those around her. She is meant to be attractive, effervescent, and just the right size—not too big and not too small—while making all of this seem effortless. And if she wants to win some extra brownie points, she learns how to embody a "cool girl" persona. A lady in the streets, and a freak in the sheets.

But growing up in a society that has never taught her to prioritize her own pleasure often causes her "freakiness" to be a bit performative.

The truth is, embodying the role of a woman can often feel like a minefield of these types of performances. Plagued by the feeling that we're forever falling short of who we're supposed to be, attempting to be loved and accepted by those around us—without ever truly understanding what it means to love and accept ourselves. And while I think codependency is certainly just as prevalent a behavior pattern in men as it is for women, the particular configuration of pressures placed upon women make the nuances of how we heal from codependency a bit more gender-specific. Since I have only had the felt experience of walking the path of healing as a woman, I feel especially well versed with that particular healing journey. Most of us have a baseline awareness of the ways women have been harmed by living in the current structure of a patriarchal society. But to truly understand how codependency has evolved for women, it becomes necessary to unpack some of the multi-generational pain points we've inherited from our mothers.

The Patriarchal Mother Wound

When most people hear the term *patriarchal mother wound*, the immediate assumption is that it's articulating all of the ways women are wounded by their mothers. My mother would probably say something like, "Here we go! It's time to blame the mother!" But the truth is, a conversation about the mother wound is quite the opposite. Our mothers are not villains. They have been harmed just as much as we have by the societal conditioning that taught them to use self-abandonment as a form of survival. Many of our mothers loved us fiercely, but their love came in the packaging of the cultural context of what they understood women needed to be. For a woman to survive in a society that demands she be sweet and self-sacrificing, make the impossible seem effortless, and require very little time and space to explore her own sense of aliveness, she must separate herself from a very fundamental aspect of who she is—the feminine parts of herself.

The patriarchal stain of the mother wound is present in the relational dynamics between most mothers and daughters to some extent. This wound is passed down generationally by women who have internalized negative or disempowering beliefs about women to their daughters. As bell hooks so aptly pointed out in her book *The Will to Change: Men, Masculinity, and Love*, "Most of us learned patriarchal attitudes in our family of origin, and they were usually taught to us by our mothers."[2] From what I've observed in my work with clients, the nuance of how this programming is passed down can vary a bit based on culture, but is almost always a consistent theme in the mother/daughter dynamic.

For instance, Lucy, a thirty-six-year-old first generation Asian American client of mine, consistently struggled with the acceptance of her viability as a financially independent single woman. Whip smart and deeply intuitive, Lucy knew how to trust herself the moment she stepped into a board room. She would recall for me with extreme delight her unique gift for cutting her older, chauvinistic coworkers off at the knees by pointing out the discrepancies and limitations in their archaic ideas of how our society and businesses should function. I remember feeling so empowered and proud to be a woman as I listened to her recount details of the victorious exchanges she'd had during her work week.

When it came to her personal life, however, Lucy's persona took on an entirely different flavor. Being a single woman in her mid-thirties often left her feeling inept and insecure amongst her peers, who were focused on their married lives, mortgages, and preschool admission sagas. The flames of her insecurities were often fueled by conversations she had with her own mother. Lucy lamented that no matter what she achieved on her own, her mother had no interest in discussing anything other than the status of her romantic and family prospects. One day she mentioned to her mother that she was thinking of buying a condo, given the exorbitant amount she was spending each month on rent when she could be building equity in a property she owned. Her mother scoffed in disgust. "No man is ever going to want you if you continue to point out that you're perfectly fine on your own."

Lucy often recalled the immense financial insecurity she experienced in her home growing up. Her parents both worked incredibly hard to give their two children every opportunity to fit in with American culture, prioritizing the importance of getting a good education above everything else. Although it was always clear to Lucy that her mother was the one more suited to managing the larger financial vision for the family (by compartmentalizing and stretching the money that they had), the financial responsibilities always fell on her overwhelmed and anxiety-ridden father. This was the role that Lucy had learned from her mother was a man's role to play—just as Lucy's mother had more than likely been taught the same thing by her own mother. Lucy lived, as so many modern women do, in a constant state of conflict between what it would mean to stand unapologetically in her power as a woman, and longing for a partnership that might require her to downplay her capabilities in order to adhere to the societal expectations set out for women.

Even if our mothers attempted to give us space to forge our own path, we can often still feel haunted by our inability to flawlessly execute the roles of womanhood that our modern society demands of us. Joanna, another client in her mid-thirties, seemed to the outside observer to have it all. She grew up in a Midwestern, White Anglo-Saxon family with a fair amount of privilege, attended an Ivy League school, married her college sweetheart, and initially came to see to me about a consistent sense of malaise about her life in its entirety. Yes, the challenges of attempting to juggle a high-power job, two young children, a marriage, and all the day-to-day tasks felt taxing—but her baseline sentiment of discontent had a slightly different flavor than that of overwhelm.

Joanna's mother had been a homemaker, completely devoted to her role as a wife and mother. From Joanna's perspective, her mother was a bit subservient to her father in a way that made her uncomfortable. Her mother often commented that she was so proud that she'd raised a daughter who was doing what she herself had longed to do but hadn't had the opportunity to experience. This was a consistent theme throughout Joanna's childhood. "You can do anything a man can do. You can be anything you dream of being. You can literally have it all!"

But somehow in the quest for having it all—often in response to the opportunities she knew her mother had missed out on—Joanna realized she hadn't ever learned to identify the things that actually brought *her* a sense of joy. She was clear about the blueprint of what society deemed to be a successful life. But finding herself smack dab in the middle of everything she'd been conditioned to achieve, she couldn't help but find herself asking in all sincerity, "Is this all there is?" If I had a dollar for every woman I've seen grapple with a similar inner conflict to Joanna's, I'd have a nice little chunk of change by now.

I can intimately recognize the impact of my own mother's patriarchal wounding on my unconscious choices. There was certainly a generational pressure to live up to a certain standard of who I was meant to become. The cultural context of my own mother wound came with the tension of pushing against the negative stereotypes society holds about Black people. My mother (like her mother, and her mother's mother) had assimilated into a way of being Black women in a culture that rejected every part of who they were as a means of survival. Survival for Black women, in a society that does not recognize or allow space for their feminine essence; strips them of their Black male counterparts through dehumanization and systemic racism, thus forcing them into a state of mandatory independence; and places them at the bottom of each intersectional hierarchy has meant that there is one characteristic above all others that Black mothers must teach their daughters to value: strength.

I was taught that being a strong Black woman meant pushing against the negative stereotypes society holds about Black people. This looked like attempting to fit in—but never in an attention-seeking, loud, or boisterous way. It meant emulating White standards of beauty and excellence—like straight, flowing hair; a petite frame; educational capability; and various demonstrations of good parentage, as well as pushing back against the most prominent archetypal assumption made about Black families—the archetype of the broken home. Reflecting on this cultural pressure helped me see that for my family, my beautiful wedding day represented so much more than a ritualistic rite of passage or the joining of two families together in a sacred union. It represented a sense of accomplishment and a momentary experience of being a "good enough" Black family.

Since becoming a therapist, I've come to understand that this "model minority" paradigm exists within the cultural experience of several marginalized groups. It's actually an unconscious attempt to blend in and maintain a sense of safety in a society that is continuously minimizing your humanity. Black mothers—mine included—are often desperate to provide their daughters with the best life possible, given the hand that they will inevitably be dealt. This is how they love them—by teaching them how to survive in a world that they know will certainly reject them. They teach them to survive, but certainly not how to embody an authentic sense of Self.

An Inconvenient Truth

So, here's something I've noticed about therapists. From what I've experienced, couples work can be a bit polarizing. Therapists tend to either absolutely love working with couples or refuse to work with them altogether. As someone who works predominantly with couples, I've often had a difficult time finding referrals for couples. I think this is because most of us (even those who are trained to support others in conflict resolution) tend to feel a bit activated sitting in the presence of extreme conflict. And most people (at least historically—this has changed a bit) initially come to couples therapy when they're in the midst of relational crisis. Sitting in this type of emotional activation can feel deeply confronting for all of us. We are forced to face some of our own programmed illusions around love and relationships.

Personally, I love working with couples. Mostly because I don't believe the goal of couples therapy should be salvaging a relationship between two people. To me, the work is more about supporting people in living the most authentic, beautiful lives they possibly can—even if that means the dissolution of their relationship. I know, unpopular stance, but it's the hill I'm willing to die on. And I've found that holding the work in this way allows me to bring a lot more presence into couples work. Presence that I might not have if the main goal were attempting to save the relationship.

Doing this work has helped me see certain aspects of romantic love with a particular amount of clarity. Here's a few of the things that I've discovered: First, most of us were conditioned to believe in an incredibly transactional, codependent model of relationships. This model, in my opinion, has very little to do with actually loving another person well. I've come to believe that love is much more about healing and witnessing another in the highest truth of who they are. Second, our great-grandparents' model of marriage and partnership has become antiquated and unsustainable, in a society where our options are unlimited and instant gratification is the norm. And last, the "happily ever after" marriage model that our patriarchal society has served up as the baseline of a dream come true is a RAW DEAL for women.

We're taught to covet the idea of being **chosen**. Being someone's one and only. To long for a big fancy ring, spend months preparing for the one day when we will get to don a gorgeous white dress, be the center of attention, and proclaim our love in front of a large group of dreamy-eyed witnesses. But we're not taught to be curious about what comes next. As I mentioned earlier, a marriage ceremony is one of the few initiatory rituals our society has left. When we were a more collectivist society, we used to honor the importance of rituals. We used to lean upon our elders to usher us through these thresholds of initiation. We understood the impact it has on the psyche when we leave one life stage behind to enter another. And we held the decision to step over these thresholds of initiation with a deep sense of reverence and respect.

I believe some part of us knows that these rituals were meant to be about much more than perfect venues, seating arrangements, who makes the cut as a bridesmaid, and choreographed dance routines. Especially because all of this "to-do" is literally about one day of our lives—which incidentally goes by in a flash.

Couples tend to come see me for therapy around four to six months after the honeymoon. When the euphoric buzz of attention has died down, and the conversation has inevitably shifted to when the first baby will be arriving. When they're starting to notice that getting along is much more difficult than it used to be. And here's the kicker—when the woman is starting to feel a twinge of resentment or contempt as she gazes over at her partner. They're both puzzled by this because she hadn't felt this resentment before.

Here's what I've come to understand this twinge to be about. After a while, a married woman starts to settle into the realization that she is no longer feeling seen and pursued. She is now someone's wife—a possession, a role to be played. And in today's society, that quite often means being a substantial contributor to the household income while simultaneously continuing to carry the majority of the emotional labor in the home. This emotional labor often includes:

- organizing social engagements
- staying connected to extended family and acting as the matriarchal touchstone
- defending against your partner losing interest through obligatory sex and remaining desirable
- comparing yourself to other women and imagining they've figured it all out
- juggling a smorgasbord of activities once there are kids in the picture
- keeping up with the latest parenting practices for healthy development

All of this while fighting the voice in your head telling you that it's Never. Ever. Good. Enough. You're always letting someone down. You're in a perpetual state of failing as a woman.

This is not to say that men don't have their own societal expectations to grapple with—they certainly do, and we'll address those dynamics later. But the impossible expectations a patriarchal society places upon women are a vital aspect of the conversations I have with struggling couples every single day. I know these struggles all too well because I've felt them in my own life. I often share these unspoken truths with some of my single clients who long for their own "happily ever after." I'd love to say that I think they believe what I'm saying— but unfortunately, I often get the sense that their societal programming is just too thick to care.

Now, despite what everything I've just said may sound like, I want to make clear that this book is not anti-relationship. Quite the opposite. I'm a huge proponent of love and partnerships. But there are certain things that both my work and my own personal journey have helped me understand about how we are conditioned to think about love and partnership that leave us feeling deeply dissatisfied and disempowered in our lives.

It's because of these things that I ultimately decided to write the guidebook that I needed in my own relationship. The book that would have helped me understand the dynamics that were playing out between my husband and I when we first got married. The book I've often wished I had to offer my clients as I'm attempting to articulate how patriarchal wounding causes us to defend against connecting with one another. The book I looked for when my marriage ended and I was determined to set aside my ego-driven fears and hold that transition in a way that was in alignment with the type of person I want to be. And the book that might support all of us in understanding the work we've come into this life to do. Because although our codependent programming would have us believe that we are able to outsource our purpose and happiness, the ultimate truth is that we are always 100 percent responsible for the way we show up for our lives—regardless of the actions of anyone else.

I don't believe that any of the ways society conditions women to self-abandon are a coincidence. I think it's all been part of an extremely elaborate form of systematic patriarchal dominance. But the good news is that many of us are awakening to what's been so very wrong about how we've been living. And I believe that more and more of us are opening up to the possibility of another way.

The Path of Interdependence

I have come to believe the key to having more fulfilling relationships (both with ourselves and everyone around us), is understanding the ways we've been conditioned to self-abandon. But as we heal our codependent behavior patterns in a lasting and substantial way, we need an alternative path. A path that balances the need we all have to experience healthy attachments (intimacy) with the need we have for autonomy (independence). This is walking the path of interdependence. Interdependence is the relational practice of harmonizing our ability to be present in intimate connection with another person, while maintaining relationship with ourselves as an autonomous "other." To me, the path of interdependence is Soul work. It acknowledges that each and every one of us is a Soul. We are spiritual beings having a temporary human experience. And if we acknowledge that each of us came here with a particular mission for what we are meant to achieve in this lifetime, we see the purpose of our partnership a bit differently. Partnership becomes about the joining of two Souls, who are meant to support each other's mission. This is vastly different from the codependent notion that another person could, or should, ever be the source of our purpose or offer us a sense of fulfillment in this lifetime.

Don't get me wrong: We do absolutely need each other, and it's important to acknowledge what happens when we fall into the trappings of hyper-independence. We are pack animals, and there are numerous advantages that come from our intimate connections. Not only do we have the ability to support the co-regulation of one another's nervous systems, but we offer the experience of mirroring what each of us are going through and what there is left to heal. We heal a little more in every moment that reminds us that we are never alone. Additionally, the aliveness, inspiration, hope, and meaning we feel in the discovery of eros (romantic love) is the most potent drug known to man. And I wholeheartedly believe that it's possible (and have witnessed firsthand that it's possible) to continue cultivating and rediscovering the sensation of eros for much longer than our current structure of romantic love allows for.

These pages contain the breadcrumbs I followed to understand the path of experiencing an integrated sense of Self. So, here is my invitation: as you read through the descriptions of certain relational dynamics, my reflections on interactions with clients, and how the pieces of my own story have informed my understanding, I invite you to reflect on how you've experienced yourself in current or previous relationship dynamics. Try to be curious about your own blind spots and make note of the power you hold to redefine your own story moving forward—for yourself.

I heard Alan Watts say in a talk once that everyone is incredibly astute at identifying where they are being victimized, but very few of us like to take ownership of where we are making ourselves out to be a victim. The interdependent path is about reclaiming our power by understanding that the only person we are ever able to change in this life is ourselves. Both codependency and hyper-independence emphasize our desire to control external forces—either by holding them too close or keeping them away. Interdependence is about understanding where our own patterns originated, questioning whether or not they're still serving us, and then asking what might be another way of seeing each situation—so that we can stay in relationship to others, while taking 100 percent responsibility for what is within our control—ourselves.

CHAPTER 2

Nobody Forgets the Truth of Who They Are, They Just Get Better at Lying to Themselves

"some days I am more wolf than woman, and I am still learning how to stop apologizing for my wild."

NIKITA GILL

The Energy Between Sexes

i have this theory that something shifts within the human psyche the moment we fully commit to being in a relationship with another person. I've seen it happen for so many couples. People can be dating happily for years until the moment they make an official declaration that they will stay together until death. I believe this has to do with the subconscious response we have to the pain points we saw playing out in our family of origin. Like the passive-aggressive comments we heard our fathers mumble under their breaths at our mothers; we may not have understood as children what they were talking about, but we could feel the energetic vibration of their disdain. We might have also picked up on the energy of something like our mother's concern over the frequency of our father's drinking. She didn't have had to say a word for us to feel her fear, and the desperation she felt to gain some control over the situation.

This happens because we are all energetic beings. The scenarios above are examples of how we tune in to another person's experience based on the unspoken frequency we feel them emit. We can feel it on an instinctual level. It's like when you hear people talk about how the hairs on the back of their neck stood straight up when someone entered a room. This is the energetic vibration they feel in this person's presence.

I wholeheartedly believe that being able to intuitively tune in to what is happening energetically for another person has become a huge component of what makes me an effective therapist. I don't do it perfectly, but I will say, whenever I struggle to read someone's energy, I've found that it usually means they're lying about something. Either to me, or themselves.

One of the most useful ways I've found to tune in to the energy in a room is when I'm watching the elements of fear, resentment, and unspoken longings between two people in couples therapy. My job becomes sensing what's being left unsaid. From there, I attempt to interpret the subtext of what I'm hearing to help the other person empathize with their partner. At the same time, I'm supporting them in understanding why their partner's feelings aren't necessarily about them. So much of the internal conflict we experience in our romantic relationships has much less to do with the actions of our partners than it does to the resistance we feel to societal expectations placed upon us. It's like we sense that the roles we've been conditioned to play are restricting our ability to live an authentic life, and our partner becomes the most convenient place to channel that frustration. I can't tell you how often I've found myself saying out loud to my female clients, "My love, your husband is not the patriarchy!"

Most of us unconsciously repeat the dynamics we saw when we were little, or reflexively defend against becoming what we felt harmed by. I have often heard Swiss psychiatrist Carl Jung quoted as saying, "Until you make the unconscious conscious, it will direct your life and you will call it fate." I have since learned that what Jung actually wrote was, "The psychological rule says that when an inner situation is not made conscious, it happens outside as fate."[1] The point of this quote, in either iteration, is referencing the unconscious path we're conditioned to follow throughout our lives—and this is certainly the case when partnering with another person. We've been programmed to partner in a very specific way—and it's often not until we're in the aftermath of that decision that we start to question what we truly want.

Joey and Lydia, both in their early thirties, came to see me for premarital counseling. They are an example of my favorite case scenario when it comes to couples counseling: two people making the intentional decision to get clear about what they want their partnership to look and feel like, *before* they get married. Joey described feeling like there was an energetic distance between he and Lydia the closer they got to the wedding. It was like she was in a constant state of overwhelm, never wanting to have sex anymore, and always seeming to be a bit irritated with him. Joey questioned whether the reality of marriage felt scary for Lydia—her parents divorced when she was young after her father's infidelity and subsequent marriage to the woman he fell in love with. "I just wonder if she's lashing out at me because she's afraid I might do something similar to her one day," Joey said.

What was interesting was that as I listened to Lydia, I didn't get the sense that she feared the possibility of infidelity in her marriage at all. She had a lot of open communication with her parents, and (from my perspective) had a fairly integrated understanding of what had happened between them. They were young when they got married and had a baby, then found that they were severely incompatible, but both had moved on to other partnerships and had maintained a respectful friendship throughout Lydia's life.

What Lydia did seem to be describing in her experience of the relationship dynamic between her and Joey was that he had become more needy since they'd gotten engaged. Where he had previously made it a priority to take the lead in planning dates, spoke confidently about his plans for the future, and always made clear how much he desired her physically, he now seemed to have settled into a deep sense of comfort that Lydia found irritating. He expected her to take the lead in everything—the wedding plans, the social engagements, and every single meal the two of them consumed together. Instead of attempting to flirt or admire her in the way that he used to, he mostly complained about how infrequently they had sex. What's funny is that a lot of what I'm describing aren't the *actual* words Lydia used in our sessions to recount what was happening between them. She would say things like, "I feel overwhelmed with everything I have to do," or "I don't know why, I just never feel like doing it anymore." But when I would ask her specific questions about their relationship dynamic and how it was making her feel, she would emphatically respond that my instincts were spot on.

A lot of what I was picking up on from Lydia were some of the constant resentments I hear expressed by women in their individual therapy sessions. They rarely know how to speak of these resentments in front of their partners. They'll talk about them with their girlfriends, and certainly their therapist, but shielding their male partners from any direct criticism is a specific form of societal conditioning that I witness time and time again with my female clients. Women do a lot things to protect the male ego—especially when we're in the dating phase of our relationships. We'll pretend to be more impressed by them than we actually are, we'll sometimes play up the "damsel in distress" routine a bit to make them feel competent and trusted—and don't even get me started on the amount of performative sex we have, with the men in our lives none the wiser about all of the orgasms we're faking. This behavior is engrained in us early. I would also argue that it occurs instinctively as a way to keep ourselves safe. On some level, each of us knows the fundamental fear that each gender is defending itself against. Every woman is defending against the fear of being harmed. Every man is defending against the fear of being shamed. We don't have to speak about the fact that these fundamental defense mechanisms exist between us. We pick up on their existence energetically.

Joey and Lydia are just one of countless examples of the primary roadblock faced by couples, but for some reason, these struggles are rarely acknowledged or even understood in our society. There are so many ways that our modern civilization tends to believe it can outsmart the natural order of life. We believe we can have any food we want, from any region we want, any time of the year we want—without taking into account that there are certain foods humans are meant to ingest during certain seasons, based on what grows naturally in the climate they're living in.

We believe that we can disrespect and denigrate the earth we're living on, without a thought to where we'll live and breathe when the last tree has been cut down, and the oceans have risen to the point of overtaking our cities. And to me, our romantic relationships are one of the most precise examples of how we attempt to introduce logic into that which defies logic. We believe we can discount our most innate primal urges, without it having a consequence over time.

The Anima and Animus

In order for relationships to sustain a sense of eros (in other words, sensual and passionate love) they require a sense of otherness; an erotic polarity, if you will. Our society's current model of romantic partnership is one that has normalized a deep sense of enmeshment, possessiveness, and codependency. Esther Perel, an acclaimed psychotherapist and expert in the realm of sex and relationships, writes in *Mating in Captivity*: "Love rests on two pillars: surrender and autonomy. Our need for togetherness exists alongside our need for separateness. One does not exist without the other. With too much distance, there can be no connection. But too much merging eradicates the separateness of two distinct individuals."[2]

The challenge with our modern love paradigm is that we've allowed our desires to be completely relinquished in service to the safety of being connected to another person. We've allowed our desire for attachment to annihilate our need for personal autonomy. This brings us back to Dr. Gabor Maté's premise of attachment trumping authenticity, and back to my perspective that an interdependent model of love is the means to restore this imbalance. But how do we get there from here? First, we have to understand the instinctual aspects of who we are and what we've been programmed to reject. Enter masculine and feminine dynamics.

Studying the work of Carl Jung, the founder of analytical psychiatry, was my introduction to the concept of masculine and feminine energetics. Jung defined these polarities as the unconscious elements that live within all of us, which he specified as the anima (the unconscious feminine side of a man) and the animus (the unconscious masculine side of a woman).

While I agree with Jung's core premise that these energetics exist within all of us, there's quite a bit more to these dynamics than the suggestion that they are the opposite gender's expression within us. It's just not that simple. Since Jung's description of the anima and animus, we have learned a tremendous amount about identity, gender roles, and the complexity of the human psyche—making elements of Jung's description of these dynamics (such as the suggestion that a woman's rational thinking functions could be coined as her animus, and a man's irrational feeling functions, his anima) feel a bit antiquated and sexist to say the very least.

Furthermore, there are nuances to the interplay between our innate longings, the things we are conditioned by society to suppress based upon appropriate expressions of gender norms, and the childhood wounds we are attempting to compensate for, that can't be encapsulated in a simple masculine/feminine binary. The exploration of our relationships in the context of masculine and feminine energy inevitably brings up a great deal of understandable resistance in a society that has worked hard to step away from limiting labels, micro-aggressions against those who've spent a lifetime feeling othered by gender binaries, or stereotypes that attempt to pigeonhole us into minimizing the vast complexity of our humanity. That being said, from what I've seen, exploring these dynamics can actually be utilized as an invitation for nonjudgmental exploration of the unconscious aspects of who we are.

Given the loaded connotation that often accompanies describing something as a "masculine trait" or viewing something as a more "feminine way of being," many often wonder if there isn't a more inclusive way to describe these energetics. The Masculine/Feminine polarities that exist within all of us have also been described in the context of Sun/Moon, Yang/Yin, Shiva/Shakti, Linear/Circular, Alpha/Omega, Logic/Intuition, Dominant/Submissive, and Ego/Soul, to name just a few. It is not lost on me the privilege I hold of exploring these polarities as a cisgender female whose particular experience of othering hasn't included gender identity. And because I understand that the labels masculine and feminine carry centuries of baggage along with them, while I will use the words masculine and feminine to explore these energetics in the context of this book, I'm going to invite you to use the energetic description above that resonates most with you as you read.

A lot of what has historically caused us to bristle a bit when we think about the embodiment of both our masculine and feminine characteristics is that our society often puts the focus on the distorted elements of these energetics. We have been trained to view the masculine polarity as inherently toxic: misogynistic, cold-hearted, and dangerous. Correspondingly, when someone asks you to think of characteristics that are inherently feminine, you might note that descriptions like weak, needy, or helpless reflexively come to your mind. But the societal framing of these inner polarities has largely been co-opted into descriptions of how these elements manifest in their most warped forms. A society that teaches us to reject fundamental aspects of who we are results in wounded representations of the masculine and feminine within.

The good news is that we are able to identify energetic patterns that tend to represent what masculine and feminine dynamics look like—both in their wounded and healthier forms. I've found that the deeper I've come into an integrated understanding of these dynamics, the more I'm able to quickly identify the energetic someone is embodying (myself included) in any given moment. I promise, you will soon start to notice how these energetics show up in yourself and those around you as well. To get us started, here's a baseline description that gives us an idea of how we'll explore human behavior through the lens of these dynamics:

Healthy Masculine Energy	Healthy Feminine Energy
• creates safety	• intuitive
• witnesses without judgment	• loving
• holds space	• playful & expressive
• present without a goal	• fluid
• integrity & awareness	• heart-centered
• guides	• surrenders
• committed to truth	• connecting
• listens deeply	• births, creates, manifests
• supportive & encouraging	• vulnerable
• faces fears/knows death	• compassionate
• humble	• sensual & affectionate
• seeks mentorship	• connected to nature
• reflective	• receives
• peaceful & grounded	• connected to Source energy
• observes beyond what is seen	• authentic
• responds instead of reacting	• trusts
Wounded Masculine Energy	Wounded Feminine Energy
• aggressive	• irrational
• stuck in mind/not present	• desperate
• cold & distant	• needy
• competitive	• manipulative
• withdrawn	• insecure—seeks external validation
• bullying	
• struggles to communicate needs	• inauthentic
	• chases love/obsesses
• has to be right	• victim
• reactive	• critical
• withdrawn—runs from love	• people pleasing
• narcissistic	• projects emotions onto others
• needs to fix	• lack of boundaries
• avoidant attachment	• anxious attachment
• afraid of failure	• fears loss
• ignores emotions	• seeks external safety

Your Core Energetic

At this point, we've established that all of us have both masculine and feminine energy within us. But each of us also has a more *core* energetic way of moving through the world. This is the energy that felt most authentic to us before the world intervened with its opinions about who we were meant to be. This is the energetic that cultivates healthy sexual polarity in our relationships, inspires us to tune into our life's mission, and represents who we are when we feel like the most authentic version of ourselves. This is our *homecoming* energy.

In my experience, it can sometimes feel a bit difficult to identify our core energetic. This is because it is not necessarily based on gender identification. Those who identify as male can most certainly be a more feminine core energetic. In that same respect, there are those who identify as female who resonate with a more masculine core. I find that it doesn't take me long to recognize the core energetic of my clients, whatever their societal conditioning has been. It has to do with their fundamental longings and how they most appreciate being seen. But here's a short quiz you can take to identify your core energetic for yourself. Once you've identified if these variables feel true to you, I find this can be a great conversation starter between friends, lovers, and most importantly, a jumping off point for the relational dynamics we will explore throughout these pages.

Are You a Core Masculine or a Core Feminine?

Without giving it too much thought, pick the answer that feels most true for you.

Question 1

A. I tend to value feeling a sense of aliveness far more than I do focusing on the bottom line. It's not that I'm frivolous or irresponsible with money, it's just that being financially prosperous isn't usually what fills me with a deep sense of fulfillment.

B. I believe that my word is my bond. When I say I'm going to do something, it feels extremely important to me to follow through. I respect myself most after the completion of a goal.

Question 2

A. I understand that life will have various seasons. I don't feel upset when things don't go according to plan and have no trouble pivoting to accommodate the situation in front of me.

B. I have a tendency to feel irritated by the emotional dramas people get caught up in. I prefer to focus my energy on the task in front of me and tend to disassociate from the ups and downs of what many might consider critical.

Questions 3

A. I feel most alive when I experience a sense of connection. The details of a goal or an outcome feel less important to me than how connected I feel to the process. One question that cultivates a sense of aliveness within me might be: does the activity I'm participating in support my feeling into an authentic sense of Self?

B. I feel most inspired by the idea of leaving something great behind with my mark on it. When I think about what I'm doing with my time, I want to look back at the end of my life and feel proud of what I created.

Question 4

A. I feel most turned on in intimate partnerships when there is a deep sense of emotional intimacy and yearning for one another. If I don't feel connected, it can be hard for me to experience a genuine sense of arousal.

B. A strong desire for another person is usually the motivating force behind my intimate connections. I feel a sense of accomplishment when I have a fulfilling sexual experience with another person, and when I feel that I've provided my partner the experience of pleasure.

Question 5

A. I feel most connected when someone I care about makes an extra effort to be curious about how I feel. There is something deeply arousing about someone having a legitimate interest in what makes me tick.

B. I feel most connected when someone I care about expresses appreciation for the person I am. It feels amazing when others demonstrate to me how much they need me in their lives.

Question 6

A. When I'm making a big decision, I tend to process that decision with others. I like to receive various perspectives, weigh my options, and get feedback before I move forward.

B. I tend to focus inward for the perspective I need. I don't shut out the opinions of others, but ultimately feel that it's important for me to be the authoritative voice in the decisions I make.

Question 7

A. I like workouts that invite a deep sense of embodiment. Working out often becomes the one place in my life where I can put down all the judgments of my body and just feel good in my skin. This is how I know that I've found a workout that I really enjoy.

B. When I'm working out, I tend to focus on results. I prefer to have a goal in mind, and I like knowing that with each workout, I'm moving in the direction of my long-range goals and bolstering the destination that I desire.

Question 8

A. I love the surprises of life. I thrive in moments that show me how much I still have left to learn, the similarities between myself and others, and being shown the natural order to the mysteries of life's unfolding.

B. I feel much happier when I have a plan to execute. A five-year plan is great, a ten-year plan is even better.

Question 9

A. In my quiet moments of fantasy, I often feel aroused by the idea of someone taking control, or even being seduced in a way that allows me to surrender to them completely.

B. I feel most aroused by the idea of being in control. I like taking charge and guiding the next steps between us in intimate moments.

Question 10

A. I like the idea of being in partnership with someone who has a solid sense of who they are and likes taking the lead. There is no bigger turn-on for me than confidence and clarity of purpose.

B. I feel most attracted to the idea of a partner who trusts in me. When someone is flirtatious, lighthearted, and goes with the flow of life, this is a huge turn-on.

If you answered mostly As, your core energetic is FEMININE.

The feminine energetic has a deep desire to explore and connect. The feminine is ever evolving, shifting, free-floating energy. The feminine has an innate ability to multitask and process several different variables at once. The feminine is the energetic that is in tune with life force energy, and in its healthiest form, trusts intuitive callings. The feminine enjoys being seen and sought after and feels aroused by the idea of being pursued. The feminine longs to be longed for. Because the feminine is the energy that connects us to the Source energy from which we originated (the feminine births and manifests life), the healthy feminine has a deep ability to surrender and trust in the natural order of life as it is unfolding.

If you answered mostly Bs, your core energetic is MASCULINE.

The masculine energetic has a focus on mission. The masculine likes to move from problem to solution and is committed to having a purpose in the physical realm. This linear energy is assertive, analytical, and committed to truth. If the feminine is the energy that is most closely connected to the Soul (spiritual realm) the masculine is connected to the Ego (physical realm). A masculine energetic thrives in spaces where it feels trusted and appreciated, and more often than not, likes to take the lead during intimacy. The masculine energetic takes the action that begins to move things into forward momentum.

If you answered an equal number of As and Bs, do not be alarmed—just keep reading!

This is where the differentiation between what our societal conditioning is and what the truth of who we are at our core is can be challenging to ascertain. We will continue to explore the interplay and dance of these relational energetics further, because these energetics are not static. Various life stages, different relationships, and embracing who we are becoming once we've sifted and sorted through the layers of programming we've been spoon-fed can completely shift the energy we're embodying in any given moment. I also want to offer a reminder of the extremely common resistance that these energetic labels can bring up for us. As we answer these questions, it's very common to feel as though they are attempting to put us into a box or ask us to conform to a certain way of being. I'm going to invite you to explore them as the opposite. This is an exploration that is constantly shifting; an opportunity for self-inquiry, and not to be held too tightly when any aspect of it doesn't ring true in the moment. The point is that a huge part of our healing journey is taking responsibility for defining ourselves *for ourselves*. This is a significant aspect of what makes the interdependent path a radically different way of embodying our human experience. It is inviting the feminine perspective into our humanity.

The Collective Rejection of the Feminine

As I mentioned, the feminine is the energetic that births. Its connection to Mother Earth and the innate wisdom of life force energy itself cannot be comprehended, ordered, matched, or contained. This is the energy that describes our essence, no matter how we identify in terms of gender. When babies come out of their mothers' wombs, they are intrinsically connected to their hunger for connection, their curiosity about the world that surrounds them, their ability to intuitively trust in what they need to survive, and their authentic connection to their heart. This is the energy of the feminine. And unfortunately, this is the energy that all of us are trained to disavow within ourselves from the moment we are born.

Every single aspect of that which has been considered "feminine" has been disregarded, oppressed, picked apart, villainized, exploited, mistrusted, ostracized, and negated by the wounded patriarchal society we've lived in for centuries. This has created a gross state of imbalance, both on an individual and collective level. The feminine is the representation of the Soul of the world. When a society allows itself to disconnect from its own Soul, it is stripped of the vital life force it requires for survival. As Llewellyn Vaughan-Lee points out in *The Return of the Feminine and the World Soul*, "When we deny the divine mystery of the feminine we also deny something fundamental to life. We separate life from its sacred core, from the matrix that nourishes all creation. We cut our world off from the source that alone can heal, nourish, and transform it."[3]

As I came into a deeper understanding of the interplay of these dynamics, I had to do a bit of soul searching around whether or not to abandon the categories of masculine and feminine all together. Because again, there is a historical connotation carried by these words that can be deeply activating for some, and even feel discriminatory to others. But here's where I've landed: I will not stop describing these polarities in the context of masculine and feminine energy, because I believe we cannot heal what we cannot name.

I will not participate in the renunciation of the feminine any more than I will attempt to experience the world around me without the perspective of skin colors, cultural complexities, Indigenous rituals, the articulation of pain points, or the examination of consistent narratives that have kept us struggling to maintain a sense of peace. We have done quite enough of that already. If we attempt to ignore these significant aspects of our human experience, we have no hopes of understanding ourselves, and ultimately healing.

Why Do We Need to Understand This?

You might be asking yourself: what do these dynamics have to do with the path of finding fulfillment in our relationships? And I've got to tell you, after countless hours of curious exploration—supporting clients with various backgrounds, sexual orientations, life stages, and pain points—I've come to understand that these energetics are literally connected to **every-thing**. Almost every aspect of the ways this society conditions all of us to self-abandon stems from a warped perspective of these forces:

- valuing productivity at all costs
- feeling shame or as though we are "too much" when we're having a hard time
- fearing failure and constantly striving to be more
- allowing stress and burnout to be a normalized aspect of our daily lives
- believing we are somehow diminished when we make mistakes or "fail"
- aggression, othering, or emotional cut-offs as a means to deal with conflict
- working at jobs we hate to accumulate material success
- numbing our pain and anxiety with an array of maladaptive behavior patterns

All of this can be traced back to programming that's rooted in a distortion of masculine energy, aka a wounded patriarchal system that teaches us to suppress the essence of our humanity. As humans, we are only capable of meeting others to the degree that we've met ourselves. We cannot stay present with other people when we've been so grossly conditioned to leave our authentic selves behind.

We live in a culture that teaches our little boys to ignore their emotions, and that our girls should be viewed as hysterical when their emotions come to the surface. One of the few collectively agreed upon outlets for men to express themselves is through athletics. But the most revered sports often have a focus on aggression, reactivity, a fear of loss, and even bullying. This obsession with competition isn't just limited to the athletic realms, or childhood, or gender. Men and women alike are taught to be in a constant state of comparison. From the new car purchased by our neighbors to the fabulous trip our ex-boyfriend just posted on social media, this leaves us in a relentless state of striving to "keep up" with what everyone else is doing. We are raised in a culture that values productivity at all costs, lending itself to rampant workaholism, an inability to be present in our relationships, and ultimately, living lives that feel void of depth and meaning.

What I'm suggesting is that the values our society prioritizes are a perpetuation of our core wounds. We are in a never-ending state of flux between striving to feel like we're enough (wounded masculine energy), or judging ourselves for being irrational, weak, insecure, and needy (wounded feminine energy). This is true for all of us—regardless of gender, socioeconomic status, or cultural background. The reverence held for the wounded masculine, and the shame experienced around our wounded feminine energy, are such consistent themes in our collective pain points that they've become the baseline through which I view the path to healing. Coming to an understanding of these dynamics completely shifted how I viewed the unconscious paradigms that were playing out in my own marriage, and has started to feel like a magical lens through which I see the challenges we all face as people.

I believe we're entering a new era as a human race—a time when we're coming to a collective state of remembrance about the ultimate truths of who we are. This is an expanded awareness that we are not the cars we drive, we are not the things we do to pay our bills, we are not the fancy vacations we take, we are not what other people think about us. We are Souls. We are the energetic force that remains the moment after we leave these physical bodies. The remembrance of this fact is the tangible rise of the feminine. The feminine is the energetic force that is in tune with the Source energy we come from. It is the energy of the Soul. And I believe that in order to return to an integrated state between our healthy masculine and healthy feminine energy, those willing to embrace the integration of their healthy feminine energetic will be the leaders in the structural shifts our society requires.

CHAPTER 3

Scenes from a Relationship

"love alone is not enough. without imagination, love stales into
sentiment, duty, boredom. relationships fail not because we
have stopped loving but because we first stopped imagining."

JAMES HILLMAN

You Belong to Me

have you ever noticed how many songs include some version of the
words "you belong to me," either in the title or the lyrics? I looked into
it. It's actually a staggering number. From The Doobie Brothers to Carly
Simon to the various other artists who've performed a song with those
or similar words, the number of love songs that include some variation
of this declaration within them is just one example of how much our
conditioned beliefs about love are based on an extremely ownership-
constructed template.

The normalization of this as a romantic proclamation isn't really
surprising, given the extent to which we're raised with the ideal that
when two people *truly* love one another, they will pledge their loyalty to
that person and that person only for the remainder of their time in this
human form. Which feels like a beautiful sentiment at face value. But
have you even given much thought to how you start to feel about most
of the things that you *own* over time? You normally start to feel pretty
accustomed to having them around. You start to have the expectation
that what you own will *perform for you* in the ways that it has always performed. You probably prefer that what you own consistently meets your

needs, doesn't do a lot to disrupt your comfort, ask you to change, or make your life harder. I mean, it belongs to you, right? You might even get to the point where you barely even notice that some of the things you own are there. Unfortunately, this type of ownership dynamic can be similar to how we start to feel about our partners, once we've reached the "you belong to me" stage of a relationship.

I used to dream about someday falling in love and belonging to someone. Of course I did. Every aspect of our society inundates little girls with extremely confusing narratives about love and romance. We've already explored how this can be a factor in our collective tendency to disassociate from an authentic sense of Self. But what I find even more fascinating about the "waiting for my knight in shining armor to come rescue me" romantic narratives we're raised with is that they're at complete odds with the feminist values that many of our mothers attempted to instill in us. It's like we were instructed to hold an impossible dichotomy within—in a way that, from my perspective, most of us feel incapable of holding.

Here's what I mean: the modern feminist movement taught us that women should be fiercely independent, but we're still considered to be a bit blemished if we reach our mid-thirties and remain unpartnered. We're certainly capable of making our own money, but society considers us incredibly fortunate if we don't have to. We should absolutely long to find a lifelong partner, but we should be sure to hide the "unpleasant" aspects of who we are from them until after we've sealed the deal. Women should fight to be a man's equal in the workplace, but continuously objectify ourselves through the never-ending scrutiny of our bodies and emphasis on our appearance. All of this contributes to a society of modern-day women existing in a constant state of ambivalence.

We're desperate to be strong, independent models for our daughters, but we're smart enough to know that so much of how we're actually living our lives is a complete contradiction to the lives we would want our daughters to live. We wouldn't want them to feel like they're constantly falling short. We wouldn't want them to have a base level of shame that never goes away. We wouldn't want them to hold their own sacred bodies with ridicule and contempt. And we certainly wouldn't want them to feel isolated and dissatisfied in their partnerships. And yet, this is the reality of how so many of us are living out our days.

By the time we make our way into a committed relationship, of course it feels nearly impossible to be emotionally intimate with someone else. We've spent a lifetime learning to disengage from the authentic self that lives inside our bodies, and it's like we have no idea who we truly are. Society puts a colossal amount of pressure on women to fit the various molds of what a woman is "supposed to" be, leaving us without any space to ground into who and what we actually *want to be* in this life. But at the same time, there is an equal level of societal pressure placed upon men to *protect, provide, and procreate* without any real understanding of how to be in a conscious relationship with themselves. Relationally, this tends to result in a constant interplay of two people fluctuating between wounded feminine *and* wounded masculine dynamics within—each longing to find relational safety and healthy polarity externally, but intuitively sensing that this level of presence is not something another person can consistently provide.

The Relationship Conflict Trifecta

Shortly after I got married, I was sitting with my new husband watching a show called *Tell Me You Love Me* on HBO. The show follows the lives of three couples, each facing their own struggles with various forms of intimacy. I remember being particularly struck by the issue facing one of the couples. After several years of marriage and kids, this couple could not find their way back to being physically intimate. It was like they had some kind of emotional barrier between them that was making sex literally impossible. After finally being willing to acknowledge it as even being "a thing" going on between them, they decided to figure out how to make it happen. They tried therapy, mutual masturbation, date nights—anything they could do to reconnect.

Back then, my husband and I agreed upon feeling dumbfounded and unable to understand what was making it so damn difficult for them. "What is the big deal?! Just have sex!!" we shouted mockingly at the screen. Eleven and a half years of marriage and sitting with countless couples later, I'm not even slightly surprised by couples living through this type of reality. It's a painfully common dynamic married couples find themselves in as they attempt to make our current model of love and partnerships work.

At this point, I feel like there's very little anyone can tell me about their partnerships that I feel shocked by. I feel like I've heard about every single type of kink, dark unspoken fantasy, embarrassing source of envy, painful family dynamic, and shadow element of our human experience—either in my own work with clients, or in something shared by one of my colleagues in a supervision group. The trouble is, we have a very human tendency to believe that we— in the struggles we are facing—are an anomaly. Part of this has to do with the ego's desire to believe that it is special. The other part can be attributed to how living in an individualistic society cuts us off from the innate sense of belonging experienced by those within more collectivist cultures.

There's a reason we feel a flood of feel-good chemicals as we hear our friends commiserate about struggles they're having within their own marriages. It helps us recognize that their struggles are the same ones we've been grappling with in our relationships. There's a reason that people feel relieved after hearing their particular flavor of pathology described by someone in a twelve-step group. This recognition that we are not alone in our experience of humanity is why twelve-step groups are one of the most effective forms of pattern interruption. There's a profound catharsis we all experience in knowing that there's nothing wrong with us for feeling the way we feel. So many of the inner battles we spend a lifetime using as evidence that we're somehow broken are the most fundamental elements of the modern human experience.

I've found this to be particularly true when it comes to wading through the exceptionally challenging waters of sharing our life with another person. It's for this reason that one of the most supportive aspects of what I do in couples therapy is to normalize whatever a couple is going through as the exact same struggles that countless other couples are talking to me about every single day. And I'm not disingenuous in doing this. There are a few specific patterns I see come up so frequently for couples that I've become slightly obsessed with getting to the bottom of the *why* underneath them. Because I can see now, there are certain aspects of mas/fem dynamics that were at the root of the disconnect I witnessed on that HBO show so many years ago. Here's what I've come up with in terms of what I like to call **The Relationship Conflict Trifecta:**

Pattern I: The Abandonment/Shame Spiral

There are facets of how we're socialized as men and women that go far beyond societal gender expectations. Some of these expectations originated within our primal survival strategies as human animals. Meaning, there was a time when the expectations of men in their communities were based on the actual physical discrepancies between men and women. Men were entrusted to use their physical prowess in the service of the community as the hunters, the protectors, and the brave warriors. For this reason, men found their sense of belonging within the tribe by diminishing the outward expression of their fear—or to put it another way, by diminishing their sense of uncertainty. If they were unable to embody these qualities as men, they were characterized as less of a man or not useful within the community, which was a depiction that inevitably carried with it a great deal of shame.

Understanding this narrows down such a clear point of origin for so much of the pressure men continue to carry today. As a society, we've continued to perpetuate a narrative around the male need for certainty by making jokes about things like men never asking for directions, being unwilling to fix things around the house until you're *just about* to call a handyman, or constantly offering solutions when the woman in their life just longs to be heard. But underneath the tongue-in-cheek nature of these anecdotes is a very real pain point that I've come to realize most men carry. There's a constant need to defend against the shame of being perceived as not having the answers. The deeper layer of what is actually being defended against is the fear of being seen or witnessed—and what that equates to (on an unconscious level) is being perceived as feminine. The feminine is the energetic that is witnessed, and able to be vulnerable.

So if the male side of the spiral is shame, the female side is connected to a primal fear of abandonment. This is a primordial fear women carry around being susceptible to harm. Women have been raped, objectified, devalued, and burned alive at the stake for the audacious crimes of nothing more than existing in their feminine essence. So much of what women have passed down generationally to their daughters are mere survival strategies in the form of creating secure attachments. These survival strategies often look and sound like how to be "likeable," how to choose relationships that provide a foundation of financial security, and (most commonly) how to outsource their knowing to the world around them—ensuring their ability to fit in. Creating secure attachments within their communities is how women avoid abandonment in a world that has demonstrated in countless ways that they are not safe existing on their own.

I watch the aftermath of these fears play out between couples constantly. Here's an example. Josh and Molly were a couple in their late thirties. These two had a solid connection, work that brought them a great deal of fulfillment, and three kids keeping them busy on the weekends—but also, so much gratitude for the life they'd built together. Molly and Josh were what I love to call a maintenance couple—meaning, quite often when they came in for sessions, they didn't have a lot that they were struggling with per se, but they found that sitting with a marriage therapist offered them a helpful third perspective in their relationship.

But there was one pattern that they periodically found themselves struggling with, and it's a common one. It plays out like this: Josh likes to spend his Sundays golfing with a group of friends. Molly supports this fully as it always makes Josh incredibly willing to pick up a bit more slack with the kids on Saturdays, and she ends up spending Sundays hanging with some of her other mom friends. On more than one occasion, however, a late Sunday-evening conflict has ensued about something small. For instance, they offered me the example of Molly asking Josh one Sunday to stop at the store on his way home to pick up poster paper for a school project that was due Monday morning. Molly remembered making a point of overemphasizing how unbelievably important it was that Josh remember, because she knew she wouldn't be able to get there while looking after the three kids. Unfortunately, after a day full of golf and beers in the sunshine with the guys, Josh came home empty handed. Molly was absolutely livid.

Their argument plays out in a typical fashion: Molly angrily rails about not being able to depend on Josh for support, when she so rarely asks anything of him. Josh accuses Molly of making a mountain out a molehill and is cold and dismissive when she attempts to plead her case about why him not getting the poster paper is actually a very, very big deal. While on the surface, each person's reactions seem like a natural response to being frustrated with a partner, there's actually much more going on beneath the surface in this particular form of conflict.

Molly feels abandoned by Josh when he forgets about her plea for support in a moment of overwhelm. When he comes home without the poster paper, she tells herself an elaborate story about how she, their family, and the responsibilities they represent to Josh ultimately make him unhappy. Josh feels shamed by Molly when she uses one specific instance as evidence that he is not a present, supportive husband. He tells himself the story that he is failing in his role as her husband and the family's provider. The shame of feeling like he's getting it wrong makes him pull away from Molly.

From the outside, it's easy to see that the story that each of them is telling themselves about their conflict is arguable at least and blown way out of proportion at best. But that's the trouble. As is always the case with our conflicts, we're never actually fighting about what it feels like we're fighting about. There's a historical context.

It taps into every bit of messaging a woman receives about how dangerous it is to be with a man who might abandon you. And there's just as much historical context in the messaging men receive about how shameful it is to make a mistake. Once we find ourselves in an abandonment/shame spiral over an issue with our partner, until we bring conscious awareness to the cycle, we're not even really fighting with each other. We're fighting with generations of pain surrounding what's been required of us based upon our gender.

Pattern 2: Invisible Labor and Resentment

At this point, most of us have heard about the discrepancies that exist around the invisible labor involved in running a typical household. But just in case you haven't, this topic has been explored primarily in the context of cisgender, heterosexual relationships, with the premise being that women are continuing to carry a larger portion of the household responsibilities than men. This topic is often discussed in terms of the work nobody's being paid for—making all the meals, scheduling all of the doctor's appointments, remembering to pick up gifts for the birthday parties, knowing which cleats a child needs for the season, keeping up the communication with Parent Teacher Associations, and so on and so forth. Personally, I like to talk to couples about this discrepancy in terms of the emotional labor carried by each person in the household, because it's not so much the tasks themselves that are causing the most stress, but the internal to-do list we're carrying around in our heads.

I've been thrilled to see this issue getting more attention, because it's one of the most common points of contention I navigate with clients feeling dissatisfied in their partnerships. But I actually don't think it's an issue that's exclusively related to gender in the way I've often heard it categorized. Yes, traditionally women have been socialized to carry more of the weight of keeping a household functioning, but I think this dynamic has way more to do with how each of us are conditioned to create a sense of internal safety. Because from what I've seen, there's usually a vast discrepancy in the emotional weight carried by the over-functioner in a relationship versus the under-functioner.

Over-functioner/under-functioner dynamics are one of the ways that codependency manifests in relationships. One person (normally as a result of the experiences from their upbringing) has been conditioned to believe that the best way to keep themselves safe—minimize stressors, maintain relationships, and make sure things go according to plan—is to take responsibility for doing *everything* themselves. The other person in this relationship dynamic (because again, we will instinctually create polarity in our relationships) will start to relinquish their sense of personal responsibility—they will assume that the other person will handle things, start dumbing themselves down in terms of what they know they're truly capable of, and essentially begin to allow the other person to function for them. This tends to create an exorbitant amount of resentment within the over-functioner—not to mention what it does to erode the erotic charge between two people.

This issue becomes far more complex than a simple need for one person to step up their game and carry more of the workload around the house. There are deeper structural issues at hand that have to do with capitalism, what we've chosen to value as a society, and a wounded patriarchal system that has placed all of us on an imaginary assembly line—in a constant state of striving for more, feeling like we're falling short, and imagining that something catastrophic will ensue if we don't ensure that our child participates in every possible enrichment activity offered. Essentially—as a society, we're over-functioning.

The current structure of our nuclear family systems are a further illustration of how much value we place on wounded masculine ethics over anything and everything that might represent healthy feminine energy. We've structured our society to prioritize power over people.

We normalize:

- doing work that drains our life force—and living for the weekends

- latchkey kids who get out of school long before their parents get home—without a community to support them

- a form of modern feminism that puts women in an impossible state of constant depletion—encouraging them to negate any aspects of their feminine essence to prove they can perform just like the distorted conceptualization of a "successful" man

- filling our lives to the brim with activities—while never questioning when enough will be enough

The more I listen to those struggling with household labor discrepancies in their partnerships, the more I see them as less of a gender equality issue and more of a patriarchal dominance/wounded masculinity issue. A society of people that don't value the feminine can't really value their own lives. Because our Souls (our inner feminine) know that when we leave these bodies, the empire of riches we leave our families will be irrelevant, how far along we got on our to-do lists will be irrelevant, what kind of colleges our children attended will be irrelevant—and most certainly, what everyone else was doing on their social media feed . . . will be completely irrelevant.

Our Souls know that most of what we spend our days prioritizing as a society doesn't really matter that much at all. At the end of our lives, what will matter to us will be the quality of the connections we had. And when we're attempting to pack our days to the absolute brim, it becomes impossible to be present for our connections. Yes, we need to lean into having vulnerable conversations about how we might divide and conquer in a way that feels a bit more equal—but ultimately, as a society we need to ask ourselves in all sincerity if we're just trying to do way too much.

Pattern 3: Parenting Your Partner and Power Dynamics

Nobody gets through childhood feeling fully seen, supported, and understood by their caretakers. In fact, whenever someone comes into therapy proclaiming they had a "perfect childhood," I guarantee you that the therapist sitting across from them is secretly smiling like a Cheshire cat on the inside. It means there's a lot of "rich grist for the therapy mill" (a phrase therapists often learn in graduate school) hidden just below the surface. Whatever wounds—large or small—we are carrying from childhood, we unconsciously attempt to heal them in adulthood. The chemistry, familiarity, and longing we initially feel for another person is usually the result of an unconscious pain point from our past. It may take a little while for the initial love bubble to burst and for us to recognize the pain point—but I assure you, it's always there.

Here's how I tend to bring this fact into the conscious awareness of my clients (if you're in a partnership, you can try playing with this exercise for yourself):

Think about some of the things your partner does that make you absolutely nuts.

Here's a few examples that come up often:

- forgetting to change the toilet paper roll
- criticizing your fashion choices
- flirting with other people
- leaving the dishes in the sink
- refusing to help plan for retirement
- belittling you in front of others
- constantly questioning your parenting
- promising you they'll handle it . . . tomorrow
- drinking too much and embarrassing you
- prioritizing football season over you
- minimizing your feelings as dramatic
- buying gifts that make you feel unseen
- leaving you alone at their office parties
- withholding or constant need for affection
- micromanaging things they ask you to do
- never planning dates or wanting to go out

Now, think about some of the feelings that these behaviors bring to the surface for you.

Here's a few examples of how your partner's behavior might make you feel:

- dismissed
- unseen
- criticized
- forgotten
- humiliated
- unimportant
- abandoned
- unloved
- taken for granted
- untrustworthy
- afraid
- alone
- unwanted
- disrespected
- unsafe
- forgotten
- overwhelmed
- used
- rejected
- overlooked
- undesired
- ignored
- degraded
- irritated

Next, think about what feels historic about feeling this way. Does the feeling that came to the surface as you thought about your partner's behavior remind you of how anyone else in your life has made you feel? Did you feel frequently criticized, overlooked, or disrespected by one of your parents or primary caretakers?

Every time I run through this exercise with a client, it's a near-inevitable conclusion that their partner's behavior reminds them of the relationship they had with **the parent they had the most challenging relationship with**. This isn't just a strange coincidence. There's a reason someone feels attracted to a person whose behavior is hot and cold after being raised by a parent who was emotionally inconsistent. There's an explanation for the propensity to choose a controlling mate when your mother's controlling nature made you feel like you couldn't breathe. There's also a reason why someone might choose a partner with addictive tendencies, when watching those same tendencies play out in their father's opioid addiction caused the entire family so much pain.

We're drawn to these partners in an unconscious attempt to heal from the things that hurt us in our past. Our inner child wants to course-correct the pain points of our past, to prove that despite the moments that made us feel unlovable, we were in fact loveable after all. The trouble with this as a healing strategy is that as long as two people are unconsciously choosing one another in an attempt to heal their pasts, they end up reenacting those pain points—an unconscious form of repetition-compulsion—continuing to exacerbate their hurts even more.

Until we make the unconscious conscious, the family systems we create through marriage inevitably recreate the most dysfunctional dynamics from our family of origin. We either look for our spouse to give us the love and recognition we didn't receive from the parent we longed to receive it from, or we find the love they offer intolerable because we've learned not to trust love. Either way, we start to resent our spouse for their inability to "meet our needs," in the same way we resented our parent. I say "meet our needs" with quotation marks because this is one of the places that I think the current perspectives of relational therapy are missing the mark just a bit. If the goal of our lifetime is to become a more actualized version of ourselves—essentially to return to an awareness of our innate wholeness—we are challenged to see that our partnerships can either serve as a vivid mirror that propels us into deeper layers of healing and self-awareness, or a convenient space to distract ourselves from taking personal responsibility for our growth and inner work.

Margot and Roshawn were a classic example of how parentified dynamics start to become problematic in partnerships. Both in their mid-forties, they had each achieved a great deal of career success but were struggling with a lack of connection in their relationship. Roshawn had been a child actress—she'd hit the peak of her success in her early twenties, spent the majority of her thirties attempting to get clean and sober, and then found a deep sense of grounding and safety when she met and married Margot in her early forties.

Roshawn joked frequently that Margot was "the adult in the relationship." This was not a new phenomenon for Margot, as she had spent a lifetime being the adult in her relationships; first, with her single mother (picking up the slack and helping her keep the lights on), later on as the "mother figure" to all of her friends, and then in every relationship she'd ever had prior to meeting Roshawn.

Margot was a self-made woman. She prided herself on the fact that everything she'd built, she'd built by herself—and while she wanted Roshawn in her life, she most definitely did not need her. When she first met Roshawn, she found her effervescence endearing and that it somehow gave her an ability to access her own lighthearted energy. But lately, Margot had been seriously questioning if this was the right partnership for her after all.

Margot described Roshawn as lacking a sense of purpose in a way that was increasingly feeling like a turn-off. The issue of purpose didn't have anything to do with money; Roshawn had plenty of financial resources, and Margot's company was actually thriving in the midst of the pandemic. "She spends her days . . . I don't even know, what do you do all day? Just hang by the pool? Play the guitar? I didn't even realize it until I was working from home, but she literally doesn't do anything! And she wasn't like this when we first met. She was so into her twelve-step program and helping other people. I used to feel inspired by everything she had going on. Now, she just acts like it's my job to handle everything. And then she's constantly complaining that I never want to have sex. But honestly, I don't feel attracted to you anymore," Margot blurted out in session one day with tears streaming down her face, unable to look Roshawn in the eyes.

There's a few things that I could see brewing just beneath the surface that were the source of Margot and Roshawn's impasse. Yes, they were struggling with the results of what happens when one partner takes on a more parentified role with the other (again, a classic over-functioner, under-functioner polarity), but on a deeper level, these issues had to do with masculine and feminine dynamics. Margot was a core feminine, but after a lifetime of learning to depend on herself, she had developed a pretty solidified wounded masculine armor. The same survival skills that made her an incredibly successful businesswoman—competitive, able to tackle adversity, quick to brush off her emotions, and deferring to logic as her first response—had made her numb to some of her most innate feminine longings. I would ask Margot questions like:

- When was the last time you danced? Do you like to dance?
- Where do you feel like the most authentic version of yourself?
- Who do you feel like you're able to be vulnerable with?
- What does the word *surrender* bring up for you?
- When do you feel the most beautiful?
- When was the last time you felt fully able to receive support?

These questions went from eliciting a sense of hysterical laughter, to deep irritation, to an overwhelming sadness within Margot. These questions highlighted that as I suspected, Margot had been disconnected from the elements of her feminine essence for so long that hearing me talk about them made her feel like I was poking at something she'd rather I not poke.

The wounded masculine energy that Margot was embodying in her relationship with Roshawn was a progression of the mothering role she'd taken on so many times in her life. We'll talk more about the linear, solution-focused, masculine energy that motherhood brings forward in a core feminine when we talk about parenthood, but the pain point that caused Margot to act out this energetic in her partnerships has to do with her being a parentified child.

The survival strategy of parenting those we care about isn't unique to parentified children (meaning children who were forced to take on more of a parental role with their caretakers from a young age)—this is also a fundamental attribute of codependency. In codependent dynamics, we solidify our connection to another person by making sure they need us. We don't do it consciously, but in the same way that a parentified child receives a hit of self-worth each time their parent praises them for their ability to handle such grown-up tasks, finding a partner who needs you (and will thus never abandon you) can create a feeling of safety in the earlier stages of a romantic attachment.

But overly parentified dynamics between two adults are never sustainable. Just as we are meant to create a healthy sense of differentiation between ourselves and our parents in adolescence, one partner carrying more responsibility, being seen as the ultimate authority, and thus stunting the development of their partner will inevitably lead to resentment in one partner and rebellion in the other.

This was precisely how the dynamic was playing out between Roshawn and Margot. Roshawn oscillated between desiring to be seen and acknowledged by Margot, then feeling belittled and infuriated by her control. It was clear to me that Roshawn was a core masculine, and that living without a sense of clarity, a commitment to some sort of mission, and a sense of who she was in her own right, was causing her to feel depressed. She started to embody a wounded feminine energetic to create polarity with Margot's wounded masculine energetic, and because this energetic was inauthentic to who she was at her core, not only was this energy like a repellent to Margot (who in her core feminine essence longed to be seen and able to receive support), it also filled Roshawn (in her masculine core) with a deep sense of shame.

Incongruent sexual desire frequently shows up when we are living out of alignment with our authentic self in a partnership. This is usually the case when the desire for sex isn't stemming from an authentic feeling of connection to our partner. Sex can serve as a way to numb uncomfortable feelings (or the lack of any feelings) in the same way that we can use drugs, alcohol, or any other addictive substances. The frequency of Roshawn's desire for sex (at a time when she and Margot were emotionally disconnected) is a very common way that one person in a couple attempts to use sex as a sort of pacifier for discomfort. Because Margot can instinctually feel that Roshawn's desire for sex has very little to do with her and more to do with Roshawn's desire to feel *something*, Margot feels incensed by her advances.

But if we put aside the motivation behind Roshawn's advances, we can see that the parentified dynamics between them are responsible for the lack of erotic polarity—just like with so many other couples. We've normalized such a deep sense of enmeshment in our partnerships—feeling entitled to control one another, questioning one another's competence, doing for an adult what they're perfectly capable of doing for themselves. These are all spaces a parent might occupy, not your lover. And while a certain amount of caring for our partner is necessary and healthy, it is unbelievably common for the pendulum to swing too far in the direction of caretaking. We are not meant to desire our children. And we are not meant to parent our partners.

How It Looks vs. How It Feels

Our society loves things that look good—regardless of how they feel. We're socialized to sacrifice the truth of our experience in exchange for the perfect images we present to the world. I don't really think I had a felt sense of how rampant this societal tendency is until I became a therapist. There are so many consistent themes I hear happening for my clients. Eventually, I started to realize that for most of us, the truth of our "behind the scenes" looks very different from the "highlight reel" we present to the world. And it shows up in so many facets of our lives: falling deeper into financial ruin to maintain an impressive house and lifestyle we simply cannot afford, longing to do or be something other than who we currently are—but feeling like we would be ostracized if we took the chance and failed, or feeling a deep sense of despair about the lack of inspiration, meaning, and contentment we're experiencing in our lives on a daily basis.

As a couples therapist, I often notice this as the root of the conflicts couples are playing out. So often, two people are sitting in front of me who are deeply disappointed with what their life has turned out to be—and their partner just feels like the most accessible place to project their anger and disappointment. And here's what's so heartbreaking. Neither person is actually to blame for the lack of fulfillment they're experiencing—not really. They're simply enacting the roles that society has taught them to play. And make no mistake about it, the society we've been living in is the most quintessential example of wounded masculine energy possible. Capitalism—is wounded masculine energy. White supremacy—wounded masculine energy. Ignoring the truth of our emotions—that's wounded masculine energy. Living in a constant state of productivity attempting to prove that we're enough—Wounded. Masculine. Energy. The insistence on domination, bullying, controlling, or holding others with contempt and harsh judgment that has become far too commonplace in our culture—all of that is wounded masculine energy. America was literally founded on the premise of wounded masculine values. And it's this value system that's made sustaining fulfillment in our relationships nearly impossible.

Lauren, age thirty-three, initially came to see me in the aftermath of her husband discovering she'd been having an affair for a little over a year. Lauren had been married for a very short time when the affair began, and she described feeling as though the realities of marriage sent her into a bit of a panic—causing her to, as she put it, "Lose her mind for a while." She described her husband as such a great guy. He was deeply committed to her happiness, looked to her for guidance and insight about nearly every decision he made, and he was loyal—almost to a fault. Lauren described the feeling of hurting her husband as being similar to what she imagined it must feel like to kick a small puppy. She felt like an absolute monster.

But here is the issue I identified coming to the surface as I listened to Lauren. A woman doesn't want to have sex with a small puppy. She might really love it, she'll certainly want to care for it, she may even enjoy having it in her life and form a significant connection to it—but she certainly doesn't desire that puppy.

Lauren's predicament felt like another example of where we've decided —as a society—that we can outsmart some of our most primitive human instincts. Her husband was everything she'd been conditioned to believe she *should* desire. He was nice to her, she never had to question his loyalty, and he allowed her to lead. In fact, according to Lauren, his favorite mantra was "Happy wife, happy life." But Lauren is a core feminine woman. She doesn't have an authentic desire to be with a man who is constantly looking to her for leadership.

When she told me about the man she'd been having the affair with, it became clear to me that this man presented with a great deal of distorted masculine energy. He was hot and cold, often critical, and obsessed with building his career—which left Lauren feeling desperate for bread-crumbs of his attention. But the sex. Lauren described feeling a sense of arousal that was like nothing she'd ever experienced before in her life.

We could certainly explore (and Lauren and I definitely did explore) the attachment wounds that this hot and cold relationship activated within her. But as I listened to her describe the juxtaposition between her loyal husband and this other man, I couldn't help but feel captivated by the experience of a masculine polarity that this indiscretion created for her. Even if this dynamic activated a wounded feminine response within her, it didn't matter. She was desperate to have a space where she could be experienced in her feminine. She was hungry to be with a man who held a sense of clarity. Hungry to be taken by a partner who was unafraid to take the lead. These are some of the inconvenient truths we've been conditioned not to acknowledge as modern independent women. We've been trained to understand that any self-respecting feminist never looks to a man for leadership.

But here's the troublesome discrepancy between what empowered women are conditioned to believe that we *should* want, and what actually appears to turn us on: I've consistently heard it noted that up to 60 percent of women fantasize about being overtaken sexually by a man.[1] You can sense a flavor of this discrepancy in the fact that the *Fifty Shades of Grey* trilogy—books that depicted a young woman's experience of being dominated by a powerful, slightly older man—was the bestselling book in the United States over the past decade.[2] There is a primal desire to be in the presence of masculine energy that creates an overwhelming sense of containment. We've been conditioned to see this as a form of misogyny. But what creates a sense of polarity in our erotic longings can be vastly different from what we are willing to tolerate in several other facets of our lives.

There is an absolute epidemic of women having performative sex in our culture. Faking orgasms has become so normalized that it's almost considered an art form. The narrative of the husband begging his completely disinterested wife for sex is literally the most common conversation I have with the couples I see. And I can't tell you the number of times I've heard women dismissively talk about the fact that sexual desire is just something they no longer experience at all. I believe this is because, as American research professor Brené Brown so often astutely points out, we cannot selectively numb. When a society conditions us to disconnect from our healthy feminine energy—our sensuality, our connectedness, our vulnerability, and our ability to receive—it inevitably creates the sensation of being numb to the experience of desire.

Wounded masculine energy is concerned with how things look. Healthy feminine energy is focused on how things actually feel. And this can be a challenging distinction to differentiate for ourselves. Because it feels good to be admired for having what society tells us we *should* want. Our ego gets a tremendous surge of satisfaction from the sensation of being revered or enviable. I'd be lying if I didn't admit that there was a part of me that used to feel a sense of accomplishment in having a marriage that was perceived as enviable or what other people might describe as #couplesgoals. But the little hits of satisfaction my ego got in those moments of societal acceptance never outweighed the nagging sense of discontent I was feeling on the inside.

We Are Not Enemies, but Friends

So what exactly is the current iteration of the American Dream as we've been raised to understand it? It looks like some version of a "happy enough" childhood, attending college in an attempt to ensure you can find a job that offers a sense of fulfillment, meeting someone you want to share your life with, saving up to buy a home, having a couple of kids, saving up for retirement, and eventually, spending your Sundays in a rocking chair before a large family dinner, watching your grandkids play in the front yard. We're taught to hold this vision as the "normal" idea of what people should want for themselves. Except, there are unspoken variables in between birth and the rocking chair that make this vision a bit more complicated for most people. These variables are elements like multi-generational trauma, a society that has forgotten how to hold space for one another and value authentic connection over appearances, a severe deficiency in elders to guide the younger generation (and a lack of reverence for the elders we have), and a capitalist agenda that requires the perpetuation of a "never enough" narrative keeping us in a constant state of productivity.

In the book *The Hero's Journey: Joseph Campbell on His Life and Work*, Campbell notes, "The first function of mythology is showing everything as a metaphor to transcendence."[3] The thing that made me fall in love with depth psychology as an approach to understanding the human experience was the use of myths, dreams, metaphors, images, and archetypes to make sense of the human pull toward transcendence. It gives us a way of zooming out on the chaos of our day-to-day lives and understanding what's happening. When we're in the midst of our unspeakable challenges—a dysfunctional family system, devastating heartbreak, or feeling like our life is an uninspired rat race—life just feels messy. It feels like we can't see any rhyme or reason for the mess. With some distance, acceptance, and perspective, however, we're usually able to ascertain a clear picture of why there is value in even life's most arduous moments. We start to see that there is a synchronicity to life as it's unfolding. This is what it means to view our lives through the lens of our Soul. We start asking of life's most difficult moments "What has this moment come to teach me?" instead of "Why is this happening to me?"

Once I started seeing couples work—and the American Dream that so many were having their own unconscious reckoning with—through the standpoint of what their Souls might be attempting to transcend, my work drastically shifted. And yes, at first it may seem like a bit of an esoteric lens to bring to couples therapy, but ultimately, I believe there is some form of existential questioning underneath everything we're grappling with. Exploring partnership this way is a significant departure from the ego-driven lens through which we're taught to experience marriage. The lens of the ego is the one that cultivated phrases like "Happy wife, happy life." Or "One person in a relationship always loves the other person more—be the person who loves less." Or referring to your partner as "the old ball and chain." You might find these expressions harmless at face value. But I see them as further illustrations of how we've been conditioned to normalize our marriages eventually turning into an adversarial battlefield. What begins as an increased sense of comfort and familiarity in our relationships often expands into a sense of entitlement, ownership, and taking the other person for granted.

We've all experienced how common it is for of a group of women to one-up each other with accounts of whose husband is the most useless, or the archaic misogyny of "locker room talk" being normalized as a means of fitting in with the guys. I can't tell you how often I reflect as I listen to couples (and I was certainly guilty of this in my own marriage) on the extent to which we would never speak to (or about) a friend in the same way we do about our partners. We ruthlessly keep score. We withhold and don't communicate our resentments until they've reached the point of an explosion. We take for granted that they will stand by us no matter how harsh our interactions become. And we normally lead with the least generous interpretation of their intentions that we can possibly find.

I believe there's two reasons we do this. First, as we talked about previously, our romantic relationships tend to bring up the most visceral experiences of our childhood pain points. Our most solidified defense mechanisms are triggered. And then anytime we're keeping score, seeking external validation, assuming the worst, or fearing loss, we begin to embody wounded feminine energy in our partnership dynamic. A healing response to feeling insecure would be for us to do some re-parenting work in the moment—or as I like to think of it from a masculine/feminine dynamics perspective, to allow our healthy masculine energy to hold space for our wounded feminine. This containing energy becomes our way of reminding ourselves that we have our own back; that we are seen, appreciated, and valued by ourselves; and that there's nothing we ever have to do in this life to be worthy of love.

The second reason we immediately jump to an adversarial position with our partners is that we've been so conditioned to allow our ego to take the lead in our decision-making processes. Our ego mind is the part of us that needs to defend itself at all costs. The ego is like a savage dog desperately searching for a way to find fault with another. The ego is the energetic that attempts to keep us safe—by consistently offering the suggestion that we are not. I love the way that one of my favorite spiritual teachers, Wayne Dyer, used to put it: "E-G-O. You Edged God Out."[4] Anytime our ego makes us feel defensive, like a bully (even if only in our heads), compelled to withdraw, or as though someone should be able to anticipate desires we haven't clearly expressed, we are embodying wounded masculine energy in our partnership dynamic. A healing response to this activation would be to meet the moment with curiosity and compassion. If we were to take the vulnerable step of owning how strong our desire was for a particular thing, and (this is the important part) *why* this desire means so much to us, this would create an opportunity for connection, receiving, and the building of trust between both partners. This is the tangible work of allowing our healthy feminine energy to step in for and hold space for our wounded masculine.

Unfortunately, when we allow these seemingly small conflicts to take the lead in our connections, what starts off as a practice of withholding from one another in the dating phase of our relationship ends up as partners who've created a huge gap between themselves that continues to build over time. We can see these patterns as what partnership inevitably looks like in a society conditioned to hold a fundamental lack of trust for the people we are meant to love, *or* (and this would certainly be my preference) we can see our partnerships as inevitable activation points— inviting us to transcend the wounds we've been scarred by, and practice moving into deeper phases of healing.

CHAPTER 4

Vigorous Honesty

"when one is pretending, the entire body revolts."

ANAÏS NIN

Children Bring a Black Light

in my experience, there's a collective idea that when two people have a baby, their lives inevitably shift into "you, me, and baby makes three" in a way that creates an even deeper bond between the couple. But it's usually not that simple. And listen—in some ways, and in certain couple dynamics, I think it does. There's certainly a deeper sense of attachment that a mother feels towards her partner, mostly from a survival standpoint, when she realizes the enormity of the challenges early motherhood presents. But from what I've seen (and certainly experienced personally), there's often an almost staggering resistance that a woman feels to physical intimacy with her partner after she has a baby. It can feel nearly impossible to shift her mindset back and forth from "being a mama" to "being your mate," and from what I've witnessed, the mere suggestion of it can often bring forward sensations of aggression and resentment. Now of course, this isn't the case for all women. But after hearing so many couples describing their experience of this dynamic, I couldn't help but sense that there's something more than postpartum exhaustion going on here.

It wasn't until I had a baby myself that I realized: early motherhood was one of the strongest sensations of being in masculine energy I'd ever experienced. That feels counterintuitive, right? We assume that in the early stages of motherhood, women would be drowning in the nurturing, connected aspects of our feminine essence. But ask almost any woman who's given birth to a baby what her first instinctual response is the moment that baby comes out of her body. She will tell you that she suddenly has a laser-focused need to protect that baby at all costs. This becomes her mission. Early motherhood is all about creating a safe container, tackling the next designated task, the vigorous assignments of sleepless nights and endless responsibilities, selflessly giving of yourself to care for the life you are charged with protecting, and delegating assignments to those around you. This is an extremely linear, structured, dominant, *masculine* time in a woman's life. The last thing in the world new mothers are normally concerned with is receiving. The last thing a new mother feels like she has time for is free-flowing, sensual energy. Question a new mother's sense of authority when it comes to her child, and you might certainly experience what feels like you've stepped in the ring with an angry bull. It's actually very common for the magnitude of responsibilities included in early motherhood to make a woman feel a complete disconnect from her feminine.

But here's the other thing that's so interesting about this time. The need for a mother to inhabit an extremely masculine function during early motherhood was not always the norm. This is another area where our current nuclear family structure has decided we can outsmart some of our most primal human instincts. In more collectivist societies, a community of women would surround a mother in her postpartum period. The elders, aunties, sisters, and friends all played a vital part in welcoming a newborn baby into the village—not only giving this child a strong sense of belonging to the larger whole, but also in supporting the mother in caring for her child, so that she had ample time to heal physically during the cataclysmic mental shift that occurs when transitioning from a maiden to a mother.

The United States is the only high-income country to not offer maternity leave on a federal level. Paid leave is guaranteed in 178 countries, the United States not being one of them. And since only 12 percent of women in the private sector have access to any sort of paid maternity leave, many women are forced to leave their newborns far earlier than is ideal—during what is known as the *fourth trimester*, or the external womb space of connection created in the first few months between a mother and child.[1] The pressure to "get back to normal" puts a tremendous amount of additional stress on a mother's nervous system at a time when every part of her natural instincts are telling her that she is meant to stay close to and protect her child.

Of course, women would experience postpartum anxiety and depression at staggering rates in a culture that sets them up for overwhelm during the most destabilizing change most of them have ever experienced. And no matter how well-meaning and sincere the efforts put forward on the part of her partner, it almost never feels like enough. The challenge is too big, the hormonal shifts too all-encompassing, the pressure that is placed on a nuclear family far too great for two people to handle alone. The woman will often experience her partner as inept, unhelpful, and another source of stress in her life. And as for that woman's partner, they often feel a strong sensation of abandonment. They too feel as though they are awkward and unnecessary in the early stages of parenthood, but with a partner who is suddenly consumed with someone else—meeting any and all of their bids for connection with a strong sense of exasperation and rebuff.

I like to normalize for couples that the first two years of parenthood are usually extremely taxing on a relationship. I don't think people speak openly enough about the toll this time takes on a partnership. And from what I've seen, it not only leaves couples feeling like they are failing, but often the rifts created between them during this time can be extremely challenging ruptures to repair. When the woman having a baby is a core feminine and her partner is a core masculine, her increased sense of overt masculine energy can create what feels like a battle between two alphas in one household. And yet, some part of her instinctually feels like something isn't right. Yes, the innate urge to withdraw from physical intimacy and protect her offspring for a period of time is a natural response to procreation, but the oversaturation of masculine energy created by the solitude of early motherhood in our current societal structure is unnatural.

I often share with mothers that as an extremely introverted person, I've never felt a stronger intuitive desire to be around other women than I did after having a baby. Some part of me knew that I wasn't meant to go through this transition alone, and I felt so unbelievably comforted when I listened to other women share about navigating early motherhood. Their words felt like a lighthouse guiding me through a directionless phase of my life. Sustenance filling me up and tuning me into some sort of innate feminine wisdom.

I have since come to understand that I am far from alone in experiencing the transition from maiden to mother as a stark internal reckoning with our relationship to the feminine. It is such a perplexing juxtaposition to feel hopelessly in love with the tiny little human you have literally manifested into existence, while also feeling hopelessly at odds with the intuitive guidance system within you that made such a miracle possible. There's something about witnessing and being an intrinsic part of the manifestation of human life that cultivates a pull toward returning to the feminine elements of the Self. There's an inability to stay comfortably disconnected, a desire to hold with reverence the complexity of what the female body is capable of, a need to receive support in a way that may not have been previously required, and a longing to surrender to the complexities of life's challenges with a different level of humility.

I like to think that if couples understand that early parenthood can make cultivating a healthy sense of polarity even more difficult, they're not only prepared to make sense of the distance once it's created, but this understanding can also serve as a way of intentionally bringing healing into some of the challenges of modern partnership that we've discussed. Attempting to maintain connection while parenting offers couples an invitation to take a long, hard look at what they're prioritizing and why. It can offer a bridge to prioritizing community support in our lives and dispel the illusion that any of us are better off when we're living our lives on an island. But most importantly, it can usher presence back into our relationships, at a time when far too many of us have become accustomed to living the majority of our lives on autopilot. If we're willing to see them as such, our children become these profound little mirrors, asking us to get very clear about the values we want to model for them. And upon their arrival, they quickly shine a black light on everything we've previously been able to sweep underneath the rug.

Our Souls Design Wake-Up Calls to Bring Us Back to Life

Our society is filled with experts offering extremely rational reasons as to why it is not safe to trust our own internal navigation system—or as it's more commonly referred to, our intuition. We've been convinced that if it can't be quantified, studied, or given a scientific explanation, it must not be plausible. But our intuition is the aspect of our human experience that cannot be studied. It's the part of us that feels a little uneasy when something in our lives is out of alignment. It's why you'll hear people say things like, "Some part of me just suddenly knew something was going on," after they uncharacteristically look at a phone bill and discover that their spouse has been having an affair. Or, "I don't even know what made me go back in the house to be sure I turned off the stove," when someone realizes they've just avoided something that could have been catastrophic.

Our intuition is the voice in our head that has a sudden knowing or insight about something—without a rational explanation for how or why we know. And the truth is, our intuition often manifests in various forms beyond the voice in our head, often moving further into our bodies. But normally, by the time our intuitive nudges have manifested in our bodies, it's because we've been shutting down our inner knowing for so long, we can barely hear its intuitive nudges anymore.

This usually starts when we're little. Many of us were taught that we needed to be polite, temper our emotional reactions, or even give someone a hug despite how uncomfortable it made us feel. This programming continues as we're taught to believe that medical professionals, government agencies, and scientists know more about the bodies we're inhabiting than we ever could. And listen, I'm not talking about conspiracy theories or a general mistrust of science—we are unbelievably fortunate to have the medical and technological advances we have as a society. But we can talk ourselves out of our experience of a chronic illness because several external opinions assure us that there is absolutely nothing wrong. We're taught to believe that there's an external authority that has all of the answers. So we turn away from our bodies' innate wisdom—no matter how uncomfortable we feel on the inside.

This can be especially true when it comes to our love lives. More than anywhere else, this is where we've been programmed to get a group consensus before we form an opinion. We look to society or our peer groups to establish our idea of what *should* be considered normal, or talk ourselves out of how something feels for us because we're "probably making a big deal out of nothing," or even continue living lives that are a downright lie—because they make sense in the context of societal expectations. Don't believe me? Think back on how many times you've called a group of friends to interpret a text message from someone you're dating, instead of just communicating directly with the original source. Ask yourself if you've ever done something that made you uncomfortable while dating because you didn't want to be seen as rude, or weird, or make the other person feel bad. Or even the societal norm of talking people out of the truth of how they're feeling, because of a narrative like "wedding jitters are normal," or "women are too emotional," or even "relationships are just hard."

These are all textbook examples of ways that we've been programmed to turn away from our intuitive nudges when it comes to our love lives. And what it essentially boils down to, in the larger context of what we're being taught to disregard, is our inner feminine—because the feminine is our direct access point to our connection with the Soul. The feminine is the part of us that is eternal—that which cannot be labeled, quantified, controlled, or measured in terms of its consistency. You can't determine when you're going to receive an intuitive hit any more than you can determine the precise day and time you are going to die. There are just certain elements of our lives that defy the parameters of logic. And in my humble opinion, the attempts we've made to create precise formulas for the art of loving another person have been to our collective detriment.

One of the most profound examples I've experienced of how our bodies attempt to bring us into alignment with the intuitive nudges we are choosing to turn away from was through my work with a client named Melody. Melody was in a relationship with her boyfriend Otis for over five years. Otis was a successful athlete and had been what Melody described as her "dream man" early in their relationship. Otis took her on fancy trips, wining and dining her. They moved in together quickly, and shortly after she moved in, Otis insisted that she didn't need to work since his income could easily support the two of them. This made Melody feel incredibly uncomfortable, given her history of being raised by a single mom, with no framework for a woman being supported by a man in this way. But Otis was so insistent that in the end, she tentatively agreed.

They weren't living together very long before Melody noticed a substantial shift in Otis' energy. This was around the same time we started our work together in therapy. At first, Melody attributed Otis' energy shift to him being back on the road most of the time during his season. They went from three-hour-long phone calls and struggling to be away from one another, to Otis pulling away in a way that felt jarring to Melody. He was consumed with the obligations of his schedule, and almost seemed annoyed with her every time she wanted to connect on the phone. In addition to the anxiety that she initially sought therapy to address, Melody had started to get debilitating migraine headaches that made it feel almost impossible for her to do very much other than focus on her relationship with Otis.

Shortly after their one-year anniversary, Melody reported feeling embarrassed to tell me that she had looked through Otis' phone. Before inquiring further about what she found, I asked her to indulge my curiosity about the reason she felt embarrassed to tell me—her therapist—about looking through her boyfriend's phone. Melody described feeling like this relationship was turning her into a person she couldn't recognize. She had never been a jealous girlfriend, and felt ashamed to be in a relationship with someone she had so little trust in. The conversation about Melody's invasion of Otis' privacy is a separate one altogether, but the ethical implications of that invasion do not minimize the fact that Melody's intuition was attempting to bring her awareness toward a lack of alignment in her relationship.

While going through his phone, she had, in fact, found evidence that Otis was sleeping with several other women. Melody was struck by the ironic nature of her situation. "I'm dating an athlete who can't keep it in his pants. Jesus, could he be any more of a cliché?" I was surprised to hear a week later that after we'd spent the majority of our last session formulating a plan for Melody to stay with a friend until she could figure out her finances enough to get her own place, she had decided to stay in the house she shared with Otis. He had been flooded with remorse when confronted with the possibility of losing her and vowed to Melody that he'd experienced the wake-up call he'd needed to never take her for granted again. Unfortunately, this was far from the last time Otis would be flooded with remorse and beg for forgiveness. It became a bit of a pattern between the two of them, with Otis seemingly unable to remain faithful, and Melody unable to walk away for good.

As an objective observer, there were two things I found interesting about witnessing Melody's patterns with Otis:

1. Melody reported a constant stream of physical ailments far beyond the migraine headaches she'd reported when we first started meeting. In the five years that we worked together, she struggled through neck spasms, fibroids, kidney stones, an STD, and eventually a series of heart palpitations that made her wonder why on earth her body seemed to be shutting down in such an aggressive way.

2. The extent to which Melody seemed to believe that if she could just get Otis to propose to her, all of their relationship problems would dissolve. She attributed his infidelity to being an unmarried man, and was unwavering in her determination to forge a lifelong commitment to someone who had a consistent habit of disrespect and betrayal.

Eventually, she got her wish. Otis did propose marriage. But not before Melody suffered an emotionally devastating and extremely painful miscarriage—right after finding out that another woman was also pregnant with Otis's child. This served as the final reckoning Melody required to walk away from a relationship that she knew was destroying her from the inside out.

What became clear to me as Melody and I unpacked the postmortem of her relationship with Otis was the extent to which she had—like so many of us—turned away from her own intuitive nudges in service of what seemed to be the more rational thing to do. Each time she stumbled upon another betrayal, she would begin to formulate an exit strategy and plan to reclaim the confident person she'd been when they first met. And then her logical mind would feel overwhelmed. She would think about the lifestyle she'd become accustomed to during her relationship with Otis; she'd think about the ways she watched her mother live from paycheck to paycheck throughout her childhood; she would feel flooded with the realities of living alone and supporting herself in an expensive city. But mostly, she would feel ashamed and disgusted by the realization of her own self-abandonment and inability to find the confidence to believe she deserved something more.

Melody's story of ignoring her intuition is just one example of how we trade the truth of our authentic Selves for a sense of belonging and security in a society that teaches us to completely disregard our feminine wisdom. We decide that things like a stream of physical ailments are just a series of unfortunate coincidences, until we are able to recognize after the fact, as Melody did, that all of the symptoms—which miraculously dissipated when she was finally able to release the fear-based bond she had with Otis—are our bodies' way of rejecting what is out of alignment with our Soul. We do this because we've been conditioned to do it. We've been taught to discount a fundamental element of who we are, without ever wondering *why* we're so terrified to trust in the innate wisdom of our own Soul. But here's the good news: as long as we're breathing, our Soul offers us opportunities to continue coming back into alignment.

I've come to understand that there will be moments in our lives that we feel certain might break us, and moments in our lives where we get very clear about exactly how much we're capable of. Usually, those moments tend to coincide with one another, and require us to really listen to our intuition. In the world of depth psychology, these moments are often described as a *dark night of the Soul*. A dark night is when the occurrence of a loss, a diagnosis, an exile, a letdown, or a misstep asks us to bring the focus back to our inner world in a way that we hadn't previously been forced to do. From what I've seen, we have two options in the midst of these fated moments of darkness—we can either let them become the moment of disillusionment that causes us to stop believing in possibility, or the moment where we awaken to the truth of who and what we are meant to become by welcoming our intuitive nature.

I've often heard people say that the Universe speaks to us in whispers (this is our intuition) unless we continue to tune out the gentle nudges coming to us in the form of a whisper. This becomes the point when the whispers get a bit louder, until all of a sudden you feel like life is yelling at you to WAKE THE HELL UP. These wake-up call moments offer us the embodied sense of what we may have previously only understood theoretically: that we are in no way, shape, or form entitled to any amount of time inhabiting these bodies. But if none of this is promised, then every moment is sacred. Every. Single. Breath. Even the most painful ones have come to fill our lungs up with a recognition of the Divine. And this recognition is often how we start making our way back home to our Souls.

Some Relationships Are Meant to Expire

We live in a society that uses longevity as our method for measuring the success of a relationship. For instance, have you ever been to a wedding where they ask all of the couples to stay on the dance floor until they call out the number of years you've been together? They continue to call out years in increments of five or so, until the couple who've accumulated the most years together are celebrated by the entire room as an example of what a successful union looks like. But no one ever takes the time to ask those couples about what their lives together have actually felt like. No one asks if there's been a sense of mutual respect present in their relationship. Nobody wonders if they'd do it all again if they knew back then what they know now about marriage. No one seems to ponder if they've been challenged and inspired to reach their full potential while in the midst of their partnership. We don't ask couples these types of questions, because they're not the priorities that a linear, patriarchal society is taught to value. What matters most is that the structure remains intact—regardless of how those inhabiting the structure are feeling about their lives.

But what if we did care? Acclaimed marriage and family therapist Esther Perel is often quoted as saying, "It is the quality of your relationships which ultimately will determine the quality of your life."[2] If our intimate relationships end up being one of the most significant factors influencing how we feel about our lives, it would seem that experiencing a sense of authentic fulfillment in these relationships would be something our society would collectively prioritize. But I'm not sure that we do. We've normalized relationships that feel more like life sentences than something that's life affirming. A partner who feels more like an irritating roommate than a lover and best friend. More often than not, we recreate the most contemptuous family dynamics from our childhood.

Honestly, my perspective on this is drawn from the people who show up regularly for couples therapy. These are the people who are actively making an effort to find more authentic fulfillment in their relationships. We can make some pretty significant assumptions about what the felt experience is like within the relationships where people are not actively seeking to be more conscious. But the fact that people seem to be choosing to enter into committed partnerships much less frequently today suggests that the collective perception of romantic unions has created an image of them being less than fulfilling when all is said and done.

Some might suggest that this is because our cultural values have become distorted, or that people are much too quick to give up when the going gets tough—and they might be right. But if we ask ourselves what the actual purpose of partnership is in a society that is beginning to question all of its dominance-based structures—like White supremacy, misogyny, gender binaries, and socioeconomic inequity—it stands to reason that some of the historic motives for joining together in union might need to be revisited as well. If a mutual sense of dependency, the fear of immorality, and the honoring of sacred vows are no longer enough to maintain the sanctity of a union between two people, what would a sense of authentic fulfillment look like in a modern-day partnership?

I think the range of answers to this question could conceivably be as vast as the number of people questioned, but from my perspective, a sense of fulfillment in modern marriages is going to require more than the security of knowing the other person isn't going anywhere. Our modern partnerships are going to require a sense of Shakti, life force, inspiration, expansion, receptivity, and Soul—in short, our partnerships have been missing the exploration of the healthy feminine energy within. Just as we've done in every other aspect of our culture, we've normalized relationship structures that are severely lacking in healthy feminine energy. Our partnerships value safety but not aliveness. Enmeshment without sensual connection. Comfort that is often lacking in curiosity.

Anyone who has ever been married can attest to the fact that what goes on in a marital dynamic is not only unbelievably complex, but also not something that can ever be fully understood by anyone from the outside. I'm not even sure the two people in the dynamic have a full grasp of what's going on between them. I feel that way about my own marriage to my child's father. The layers of complexity that led to the expiration of our marital relationship are dynamics that each of us have worked to understand (both together and separately). But they are dynamics that can never be fully understood by anyone but the two of us. I will say that the two of us were uniquely fortunate in having the shared understanding that our relationship had reached a point where it needed to change form. In my experience, most marriages don't end with that level of mutual understanding.

More often than not, there are feelings of abandonment, betrayal, and heartbreak that make the expiration of a marriage one of the most painful experiences people go through. This is completely understandable. Not only because there's a tremendous sense of grief that the human psyche is confronted with when facing the ending of something we've built our entire life around, but also because the socialized understanding of divorce equating to a failure often cultivates the feelings of ostracism and exile from our communities in its aftermath.

The felt experience of my own marriage ending gave me a unique opportunity to take a long, hard look at some of the cultural ideas about partnership that we've been spoon-fed. For instance, what if what defines success in a relationship is not longevity, but the amount of authenticity and respect that exists between the people involved? If that were the case, my relationship with my now ex-husband has been unbelievably successful, long after we decided to end our time as husband and wife. What if we defined success in a relationship by how much it inspires us to continue growing and reaching the full potential of who we are capable of becoming?

The truth is, some of the constructs of what previously equated to a successful partnership have needed to evolve because we as a human race have evolved. We (hopefully) no longer see people (of any kind) as property. And given the influx of technological advances we're exposed to on a daily basis, we're suddenly faced with an entire world of options, distractions, concepts, and coping mechanisms at our disposal—instantly. My point is, if we're going to make a commitment to something that has the expectancy of becoming less and less engaging over time, security and morality cannot be the only motivating factors keeping our relationships intact. Because ultimately, what lies at the root of our desire for security and morality in our relationships is fear. Fear of what will happen to us if we lose the security of this attachment. Fear that we will be judged by the people around us as a failure or a bad person. But underneath the fear of exile from the collective status quo is a wounded feminine attachment. It's the part of our subconscious that still believes that being alone would mean certain annihilation, or being cast out into the wilderness of life and forced to fend for ourselves.

On a Soul level, we know that we came into this life to face these fears. We were not meant to sit on the sidelines and safely hide from our internal dragons. We are meant to face our dragons head on—to slay them if we must, so that we can continue to move forward on our own unique path. I find it so interesting that we have a collective understanding that children are meant to continuously grow and change—both internally and externally—from birth to around eighteen years of age.

But for some reason, we carry the false notion that this growing and changing should cease once we reach adulthood, and that along with a license to drink alcohol, by twenty-one you should carry a clear idea of who you are and what your life is meant to be. To me this is such a gross misunderstanding of what we came into this life to do. We are meant to be in the consistent processes of growth and expansion—from birth all the way up until the moment we take our last breath. If the container of a relationship is able to hold space for that expansion—through shared values, ideations, creativity, and mutual respect—that is when a relationship offers a sense of authentic fulfillment.

But sometimes, what once offered a sense of fulfillment changes as we change. And when we don't allow space for that truth to be normalized without it being perceived as a failure (by ourselves or others), there's a very real cost to the human psyche. That cost comes in the form of an internal deadening that manifests in the form of sorrow, resentment, depression, or grief at the realization that we've been sleepwalking through our entire lives.

One of my favorite phrases from the spiritual teachings of Abraham Hicks is when they periodically joke that their perspective on long-term relationships would sound something like, "'I like you pretty good. Let's see how it goes.'"[3] And while for many of us, this level of ambiguousness does not provide enough containment to feel fulfilling, the larger truth I believe they are alluding to is that the sense of certainty we believe we've been offered within the boundaries of a marital contract is always an illusion. People die. People fall in love with someone else. People change their minds about what they want. And sometimes, relationships are meant to expire. It's an uncomfortable truth for us to sit with, but a truth that is nevertheless based in the reality of potential marital outcomes. The resistance to opening our hearts and minds to the possibility of uncertainty is not only what causes our deepest suffering when and if these shifts do occur, but it can hold us back from facing the truth head on. And without truth, we end up swimming against life's current, making it impossible for us to be carried downstream to where we are ultimately meant to go.

Ships Were Not Built for Harbors

In a society where most of us have been socialized to reject the feminine within ourselves and others, we've become extremely inept at holding space for the vast complexity of what it means to be human. We learn to only speak the truths we believe those around us can tolerate hearing, and walk through our lives carrying the pain of believing that our authentically messy selves are too much for anyone to love. And of course we feel this way—we've been brought up in systems that teach us that there is a "normal" path for our lives to follow, a prescriptive formula for raising children well, or that somewhere there's a human being walking among us who's figured out how to live a pain-free, fully realized, perfectly blissful life. It's all just so nonsensical when we really stop for a moment to think about it. But the wounded masculine structures we've been raised with sell us the fantasy that these ideals are possible.

How often have you heard of someone who finds out that their dear friends have recently filed for divorce, then says something like, "I thought they had the perfect marriage"? What about the all-too-common sense of shame we feel when we're struggling through a rough period in our own lives—because we feel like we should have our lives *figured out by now*, like everybody else does? The truth is, these constructs aren't based on an observable reality for anyone. And honestly, continuing to hold these frameworks doesn't allow us to hold our lives with a great deal of emotional maturity. We're in a collective state of resistance to the individuation process as described by Carl Jung. As I mentioned briefly earlier, the individuation process can most simply be defined as the achievement of self-actualization through the integration of our unconscious and conscious mind. It's an ongoing process of differentiation between the collective psyche and our own, one that continues long into adulthood.

And listen: I make this observation about our collective consciousness without one ounce of self-righteousness. I am as just as prone to this way of experiencing the world as anyone else—but also, a resistance to the process of individuation quite often means that we're letting our inner child narrate our lives, instead of our inner adult. This is what a wounded patriarchal system sets us up for. It sets us up for fantastical thinking—believing that somewhere outside of us, there is a Wizard of Oz: a government entity, or a paternal authority figure, who ultimately knows what's best for us and how we should be living. And while I do believe that there's an energetic force that is always looking out for our best interest, sees us in the highest truth of who we are, and wants us to live the most embodied, fulfilling lives we possibly can, this is not an energetic force that exists inside the walls of a government agency. It's an energetic force that exists within.

We have been operating within a wounded masculine paradigm of love and relationships for a very long time. This paradigm causes us to cling to a sense of security, doing what seems to make the most logical sense, even when we've lost our connection to our innate nature and feeling fully alive. We've been brought up within systems that promise to keep us safe—as long as we stay within the confines of a mythical idealization of what adds up to a fulfilling life. This becomes problematic once we realize that each of us came into this life to define what feels like a sense of inner fulfillment for ourselves. It's like that expression you sometimes hear about ships. It says that while ships are safe staying in the harbor, that's not what ships are designed for. We've been sold a tall tale about a sense of safety that exists within the archetype of a nuclear family structure. But collectively, we seem to be waking up to the possibility that that's not exactly what we came here for.

Here is what's beautiful about anything that our human psyche attempts to suppress—nothing within us remains hidden forever. I often like to use the analogy of a beach ball. With a great deal of effort, we can hold a great big, slippery beach ball under the surface of the water in a pool for a very long time. But eventually, that beach ball is going to fly out from under the water with a great deal of force. This may surprise us and cause a shock wave to move through our nervous system. This is very similar to what happens to the truths that we attempt to suppress. A wounded patriarchal system holds little to no reverence for the elements of our internal feminine—our aliveness, our sensuality, our authenticity, our vulnerability, our play, our receptivity, and our intuition. We've been conditioned to see these elements as unruly, immoral, unsafe, and impractical.

But when we don't allow the feminine aspects of who we are to be expressed, they become the shadow elements of Self, lying dormant within the basement of our psyche. They become restless, provoking anxiety, desperate to become integrated aspects of who we are. And eventually, they come to the surface just like that beach ball—typically in extremely inconvenient, often painful manifestations that make us question how we got so out of touch with who we truly are.

Here's what's important to understand about how the societal roles we're taught to play are setting us up to struggle in our relationships: a society that teaches children to disconnect from themselves in order to maintain a connection to others, teaches them to look to another person to offer them the parts of themselves they have suppressed. This means that when we teach little boys to "suck it up," "be tough," or that "big boys don't cry," we're essentially teaching them to suppress the connection to their healthy feminine. This teaches them to move through life lacking a sense of self-nurturance and an ability to be light and playful, while promoting a disconnection to the Source energy within them. On an unconscious level, they end up believing that they need someone outside of themselves to feel and care about their feelings—in other words, they seek an external mother figure. Because ideally, a mother figure is the first experience a little boy has of a nurturing presence that validates how he feels. When we teach little boys that they are not allowed to feel, we rob them of feeling confident in their innate wholeness.

When we teach little girls to make themselves small, "be nice," fit in with the group, and not be "too much," we're essentially teaching them to suppress the connection to their healthy masculine. This teaches them to move through life lacking a sense of assertiveness, self-worth, and a belief in their abilities and their own voice. On an unconscious level, they end up believing that they only exist to the extent that someone outside of them sees them—in other words, they seek an external father figure. Because ideally, a father figure is the first experience a little girl has of being seen and valued for who she is. When we teach little girls to depend upon external validation, we rob them of an ability to trust in their own power.

I once heard a quote by Peter Crone saying, "Life will present you with people and circumstances to reveal where you're not free."[4] When we believe that we are dependent on anything or anyone outside of us to be whole, we are living out of alignment with our Soul's highest truth. Eventually, our Soul will find various ways to bring us back into alignment with the greater Truth of who we are. Any truth that we are suppressing in an attempt to maintain a false sense of safety will eventually come to the surface. We are not meant to hold onto the false belief that we are anything other than perfect and complete within ourselves. Yes, consistently evolving; yes, in need of connection and authentic intimacy in relationship to others. But the Universe will find a way to hijack any attempts we make to avoid the inevitable cycles of life that teach us about surrendering our fears in service of expansion.

Stage Two

SEEKING

CHAPTER 5

Maybe We're Better Off Alone?

"without great solitude, no serious work is possible."

PABLO PICASSO

Exile

when a relationship ends, there's a disruption that occurs in the entire ecosystem that surrounds it. Friends, family, neighbors, acquaintances—everyone scurries about the couple and behind the scenes of the breakup, attempting to get a handle on the precise chain of events that led to this relationship's demise. WHAT HAPPENED? This is the immediate line of questioning long before any sort of dust has settled. This is the question that people feel the need to get to the bottom of, as they scurry about to share the news during their regularly scheduled activities. This is the question our psyche grapples with as we try to formulate a clear and concise explanation for why two people would choose to uproot their sense of normalcy and security. This is the question we ask as we attempt to explain away the glitch in the matrix we're desperately trying not to see.

In case you're not familiar with it, *The Matrix* is a science fiction film series that began in 1999, written and directed by Lana and Lilly Wachowski. The films depict a dystopian future in which humans are unknowingly trapped inside a simulated reality, distracted while an external source of intelligence is intentionally draining them of their life force. There are many who've suggested that we might be better served viewing these films less as a science fiction franchise and more in the realm of documentaries. For those who've seen the films, thinking back on the special effects and action sequences can make a statement like that feel like a bit of a stretch. But when you think about the larger point of what the films are essentially saying about the behavioral patterns of a capitalist society, somehow the concept of an oppressive system being designed to manipulate a society of people into sacrificing their life force in service of what they've been programmed to believe is real, doesn't feel entirely off base after all. There is no greater illustration of this point than when we are suddenly ostracized from the collective perception of "normal" as we go through the demise of a long-term relationship.

We're conditioned to believe that our ultimate source of fulfillment comes once we achieve the dream life we've been taught to idealize. But if and when we realize that doesn't necessarily equate to the tangible experience of "happily ever after," we're meant to be completely devastated. Lost. Hopeless and broken. And in some way, especially in the immediate aftermath of a breakup, that's certainly true for most of us. But what we're not taught to consider as a possibility for our lives post breakup is the potential. The awakening. The opportunity to define who we are for ourselves. A capitalist society would prefer we not see things this way. It might make us less inclined to compare our car to our neighbor's fancier version if we were focused on fulfilling the work we came here to do on a Soul level. We'd be less prone to self-medicating with food, drugs, gambling, shopping, or sex if we awaken to our capacity to be and do whatever makes us feel most alive. We'd be less susceptible to the terror that comes from not fitting in if we found ourselves ostracized and yet coming to the realization that not only are we still okay, we're better than that. We might realize we've been gifted with an opportunity to come into a deeper relationship with our Selves—and this may shift our entire perspective of the world we've been living in. No, a capitalist society has no interest in us seeing our lives through the lens of possibility. We are much more difficult to control when we define our lives for ourselves.

One of the clearest examples of this that I've seen was in my work with a client named Brianna. Brianna grew up poor, and was quick to remind me of this when I described her childhood socioeconomic status in any other way. If I would say something like "struggling to make ends meet" or "limited resources," she would always correct me and say, "Dené, we were poor. Please. You can say it." After I got to know Brianna and her story a bit more intimately, it started to make sense to me why it felt so important to her that I not sugarcoat the reality of her experience. I began to understand as she described the desperate feeling of going on her third day with nothing at all in her stomach, and how that lives in your tissues and impacts the choices you make forever. The internalized shame that came from watching her single mother unable to pay the bus fare and asking several strangers to help her get her kids home was a hollow feeling that she described herself doing just about anything to avoid feeling again. It felt important to Brianna that I understand the trajectory of her journey, because when I met her, she was living a life that was vastly different from her point of origin.

Shortly after her twenty-fourth birthday, Brianna met Mac while she was working as a cocktail waitress and finishing up grad school. Mac was a wealthy real-estate mogul—warm, compassionate, and instantly captivated by Brianna's intellect and tenacity. Brianna described her draw toward Mac as not necessarily one of feeling deeply in love—she had an incredible amount of love for him, but more in the context of being mentored and guided by a protective father figure who made her feel seen, safe, and valued in a way that she'd never experienced before from a man. By the time I met Brianna, she and Mac had worked together to successfully triple the size of his business, bring two kids into the world, and navigate fifteen years of marriage without a great deal of turbulence. But Brianna came to me looking for support with navigating their divorce. Yes, she and Mac had shared several years of a close intimate bond. But for years, Brianna had felt that their partnership was more of a business arrangement than a romantic one. There was a fair amount of sex in the beginning, but with Mac at sixty-two and Brianna at thirty-nine, the two of them found themselves at vastly different life stages with immensely different desires. After trying for several years to negotiate their differing interests, Brianna had started to experience a deep longing to experience romantic love with someone else. With Mac's blessing and agreement, Brianna realized their time as a married couple had come to an end.

What was so interesting about Brianna's current situation was that her presenting issue wasn't really surrounding her breakup with Mac. She and Mac were both committed to their friendship and co-parenting well together. At this stage in her career and with what she and Mac had built together, Brianna had no issues holding her own and taking care of herself financially. Her struggles were more around the sense of exile she felt from her community. Suddenly, all of the relationships she'd built over the years that she'd been married to Mac felt very different. Immediately after they told people about their separation, a group of mom friends had invited her to a dinner to offer their support. There was an incredibly awkward energy amongst all of the other women during that predictable "WHAT HAPPENED" dinner, and Brianna felt a drastic shift in the way she was treated by everyone in their social circles from that point on.

She (not Mac—just Brianna) was immediately removed from the invite lists for the long-standing events amongst their inner circle. And the other moms at her kids' soccer games were suddenly more standoffish and less friendly than she'd experienced them being before. Even her own extended family (who'd made cutting remarks for years about her being a "gold-digger") met the news of her marriage ending with a tremendous amount of judgment and contempt.

"I feel the way I did throughout my whole childhood all over again. Like because I decided I wanted more for myself, suddenly I'm not good enough for their snooty, rich girl social circles anymore. Well, screw them!" Brianna said one day, attempting to mask her obvious hurt through the protective armor of angry bluster. "Brianna," I said as I attempted to ascertain the larger sense of what was happening for all of these women who'd decided to make her the target of their banishment. "Did it ever occur to you that the choice you've made has put a giant magnifying glass on their lives? You've told me how you and the other wives used to joke about offering your husbands the 'annual pity sex' as a birthday gift, or that you sometimes felt like you had a hard time relating to their incessant gossip, or how it felt strange to see the way they normalized being in a constant state of complaining about every aspect of their lives. You've made a choice to believe that your life can be as good as you decide it gets to be—and in making that choice, you're shining a light on the fact that they *could* make that same choice in their own lives, but they are choosing not to."

It's just like the character Mouse says in *The Matrix*, "To deny our own impulses is to deny the very thing that makes us human."[1] When a society adapts a very specific structural idea of how our lives *should* be lived, with the promise of safety and fulfillment as the payoff for living within the confines of that structure, any sort of challenge to this herd mentality of safety can feel threatening to the individuals within that structure. Meaning, if Brianna had the ability to evolve—to maintain an admirable relationship with her children's father, thus dispelling the patriarchal myth that a woman is unsafe, unfulfilled, and incomplete without a husband—what does that say about the structures in which these other women have put their faith? That question can be unbelievably confronting for our ego mind to wrestle with. It asks us to call into question everything that we've put our trust in and believed was keeping us safe. It can feel so much easier not to ask the question. It can feel safer to look away. It can make someone like Brianna feel like a bit of a societal "canary in the coal mine," if you will. But banishing that canary from your social circles doesn't change the adverse conditions the canary was sent into the coal mine to bring to your attention.

Crazy Women

There is a very specific historical response a patriarchal society has to women any time they dare to question the programming they've been indoctrinated with. When a woman decides she might be more concerned with choosing a life that *feels* fulfilling over her need to be chosen. When she starts to question the "boys will be boys" narratives that fail to hold grown men accountable for the fact that they're not actually boys anymore. When she has a biological response to being shamed for her feminine pull toward things like authentic connection, relational clarity, her ability to trust those around her, leaning into intuitive guidance, and valuing truly feeling seen. Historically, when a woman has dared to lean into questioning the systems she's been oppressed by, she has been labeled *intense, a loose cannon, hysterical, slutty, unhinged, a witch, selfish.* Or the most damaging and arguably most effective label—used not only to bring the questioning woman back in line but also to serve as a warning to any other woman who might dare question the external authorities meant to contain the feminine wilds of all women—she is called crazy.

If you want to quickly shut down a woman's resistance to any sort of unjust treatment, call her crazy. She will immediately have an instinctual response to recoil in service of her own self-preservation. She does this because of an ancestral trauma response to the fallout of women before her being called crazy, and the methods used to contain that "craziness." You can see this illustrated through a quick Google search on the history of the word *hysteria* (which incidentally is rooted in the Latin word *hystericus*, or "of the womb") and how it was largely recognized as the first metal health diagnosis commonly used to designate a woman's behavior as neurotic and uncontrollable. What's also fascinating about the characterization of crazy women and the diagnosis of hysteria is that these women were often described as having monthly bouts of periodic insanity that seemed to be activated by the cycles of the moon. Our current societal structures have conditioned all of us (regardless of gender) to hold the feminine menstruation cycles, hormonal fluctuations, and the feminine capacity to acknowledge our emotional shifts as a form of guidance from our highest Selves as shameful, inconvenient burdens that are inferior functions at best.

If we draw our attention back to the classification of masculine and feminine polarities, the masculine is often characterized in conjunction with the sun—that which can be seen in the light of day. The feminine is often characterized in conjunction with the moon—that which cannot be seen, but must instead be instinctively felt within the state of darkness. This is similar to the intuitive landscape that encapsulates the feminine within each of us. The clarity of this knowing is often impossible to see, feel, touch, or taste. These are the elements of certainty that could never be scientifically studied or proven, but their primordial authenticity simply cannot be denied.

I remember learning about the link between "hysterical women" and the early medical practices of hysterectomies that often resulted in a woman's death, and being horrified that a woman's autonomy and safety could be so easily threatened by the simple accusation that she was unhinged. And yet, as is often the case when systems of oppression remain unexamined (and when their point of origination is still largely misunderstood), much of the practice of controlling women by calling them crazy continues today. And here's the really difficult truth about systems of patriarchy and women. As women, we are some of the most aggressive defenders of these systems. Let me give you some examples. Internalized patriarchy in women looks like women frowning upon other women wearing various items of clothing that they're "too old for" after a certain age. Internalized patriarchy looks like women seeing one another as competition for men, and adapting a wounded masculine mentality of lack when it comes to relationships in general. Internalized patriarchy even looks like women categorizing themselves and other women as crazy, wrong, or too much when they finally reach a breaking point in their inability to uphold the impossible standards society places upon them.

It feels heartbreaking to acknowledge that there's patriarchal tendencies perpetuated by women toward other women—even within the field of psychology. I've been so struck by how often I've witnessed a woman be immediately dismissed (quite often by the female mental health professionals who make up the majority of the field) with the label of being manic, privileged, overly dramatic, or simply suffering from postpartum depression—when from my perspective, she is having a very reasonable response to circumstances that make her feel overwhelmed, hopeless, unseen, and disposable. With no further questions asked about her environment, her support systems, her pain points, her suppressed sense of self or deepest desires—just a diagnosis, more than likely some medication, and then sending her back to the exact same ecosystem she came from.

And this isn't me saying that these women's mental health struggles are not very real. Quite the contrary. I'm saying that as an entire society, we could stand to be much more curious about the *why* underneath the diagnosis. Are these women crazy? Or are they simply having an inevitable response to a society that demands that we suppress every aspect of our feminine in service of a wounded masculine agenda?

When women are raised to objectify themselves and stifle their voice in exchange for belonging, they are taught to disconnect from their own healthy masculine energy. This leaves them feeling compelled to seek external safety, to people please in order to maintain attachments, to show up inauthentically in relationships, and to manipulate others in an attempt to get their needs met. We have been conditioned to understand these behavior patterns as innately feminine; they are not. They are a distortion of feminine energy that occurs when women are programmed to believe that they cannot trust themselves. But because all of these distorted feminine qualities evoke a lack of safety and powerlessness within a woman, they result in a tremendous amount of self-loathing.

The ego mind will always rebel against the feeling of powerlessness and begin to compensate with the emulation of a wounded masculine armor of protection. This looks like the urge within women to ignore their emotions; be reactive and irritated, cold and distant; or withdraw from love all together. What often feels like craziness in women is actually the chaotic dance of distorted masculine and feminine polarities that occur when we attempt to act out of accordance with our nature. Point being, if and when women are acting in ways that some might call crazy, it's usually the result of an entire lifetime of attempting to be who and what they are not that drove them there.

Lost Boys

One of the greatest gifts that's come from my time working as a therapist has been the tremendous amount of healing it's brought forth in my relationship with men. Like many women of my generation, I was raised in the aftermath of a modern feminist movement that (understandably) focused most of its energy and resources on creating a dialogue about the damage that an oppressive patriarchal system does to women. I grew up understanding that good men work to understand and take responsibility for the enormous nature of their privilege, and that the emotional pain of what it means to grow up as a woman is something men will never be able to fully grasp. That masculinity is inherently toxic, suspect, thoughtless, and ultimately, always in need of a good woman to keep it in line. What I have since come to understand about this short-sighted, simplistic view of the complex nature of masculinity is that we as women often understand just as little about what it feels like to embody the skin of a man, as men understand about what it feels like to embody the skin of a woman.

For instance, it is just categorically untrue that all men benefit from an enormous amount of privilege based solely upon their gender. Men of color, men of a certain socioeconomic status, and men within the LGBTQIA+ community are just a few of the sub-categories of men that I would argue have had a vastly different experience of what it means to grow up male than that of a cisgendered, heterosexual, Caucasian man. And even then, I don't think we put enough credence on the uncomfortable truth that as a society, we send men some pretty mixed messages about their inherent value.

Yes, men still earn a substantial amount more than women, even though women make up an equal part of the workforce—but we still teach men that their inherent worth lies in their ability to provide. After all, the perpetuation of the societal tendency to poke fun of the men who make less money than their female partners still very much exists. And yes, men benefit from living in a world where no one is questioning their right to bodily autonomy—but we teach men that their bodies and their hearts are less sacred than women's when we save the women and children first and teach little boys to "man up" and stop feeling what they feel.

A few other stark realities about the value society places on men:

- In the United States, White males accounted for almost 70 percent of deaths by suicide in 2019

- Globally speaking, 75 percent of those who die by suicide are men

- Only about 36 percent of males with a mental illness in the US actually receive treatment

- Nearly one in ten men experience anxiety or depression on a daily basis, but less than half of them seek treatment

- Men are far more likely to be diagnosed with intermittent explosive disorder than women

- Men are more likely to experience physical assault, disasters, accidents, combat, or to witness death or injury

- Men make up the majority of the individuals experiencing homelessness (70 percent)

- Nationwide, the majority of the people in state prisons are male (93 percent)[2]

We teach little boys to disconnect from their hearts—and then call them toxic as grown men for doing so.

In the same way that attempting to dance between wounded polarities creates a frenetic energy in women that some might label as crazy (or more appropriately, view as a more anxious way of experiencing life), attempting to selectively numb various aspects of their humanity has left men with a baseline experience of depression; or more aptly put, a lack of authentic life force, which can also be viewed as a more avoidant way of experiencing life. The majority of men live their lives disconnected from the authentic experience of life force because they are conditioned—first by their fathers, and if not by a father figure, then by society at large—to hold their own inner feminine with contempt. In his book *I Don't Want to Talk About It: Overcoming the Secret Legacy of Male Depression*, Terrence Real points out that young boys learn to have an active disengagement from the feminine that is modeled by their fathers. "They learn that not just Mother, but the values she manifests in the family—connection, expressivity—are to be devalued and ignored. The subtext is, engage in 'feminine' values and activities and risk a similar devaluation yourself. The paradox for boys is that the only way to connect with their father is to echo his disconnection."[3]

Today's young boys are also not initiated into manhood by an established elder who takes them under his wing and teaches them to hold the complex nature of their masculinity with reverence and clarity. Instead, they are taught to embody a sort of blustering performative masculinity that consistently needs to be proven, minimizes the impact of their pain, and forces them to defend vehemently against being shamed or ridiculed. They learn this through locker room hazing and humiliation by their peers, early experiences of heartbreak they're meant to stuff down and pretend not to feel, and a society that celebrates them for objectifying women and seeking power through external subjugation, teaching them that things like vulnerability, tenderness, and longing to be seen and supported are not only the equivalent of weakness, but somehow fundamentally make them less of a man.

The current societal structure leaves men most commonly choosing between one of two options:

Submit to the societal blueprint of "normal": married with kids (**a distorted version of masculinity**)	Rebel against the system to walk a different path: fears commitment (**a wounded version of masculinity**)
• exist to provide	• objectifies others as a form of numbing
• sex as the only outlet for intimacy	• struggles with follow-through
• a practical job that provides security	• rebels against societal conformity
• constant seeking of external affirmation	• chases hits of aliveness
• inauthentic and people pleasing	• feels like a failure
• disconnected from own wants and needs	• controls others by pushing them away

While each of these generic archetypes of modern masculinity (the content family man or consummate bachelor) are held by society as viable options for men, in each case there is almost always so much more happening below the surface that has yet to be seen as a collective issue.

Henry David Thoreau said, "The mass of men lead lives of quiet desperation."[4] For today's modern man, that typically looks like a life void of any real intimacy, feeling disconnected from purpose and meaning, a general lack of self-worth, and attempting to use any and every distraction possible to avoid being present in their lives. The long, slow deadening of the Souls of men is the patriarchal wound we rarely discuss. And from my perspective, this is one of the most short-sighted cooperative failings of our time. Allowing for a society of men who are disconnected from their hearts has come with a series of significant consequences—which ultimately creates a ripple effect that impacts all of us in one form or another.

We Don't Have to Live Like This

The cultural narrative of the midlife crisis is one that we tend to speak about in a rather tongue-in-cheek way. It usually includes an anecdote about a man in his mid-to-late forties/early fifties who suddenly decides to buy an expensive sports car, make some drastic changes in his physical appearance, and blow up his life by leaving his wife and family or quitting his job and attending a series of ayahuasca ceremonies. Now first let me say, in my experience, this is far from a gendered phenomenon. I've seen women decide just as frequently at this midpoint in their life that they no longer wish to continue living a life that is fundamentally lacking in fulfillment. And I think there's a dismissive quality to the way we speak about and view both this midway point and the courage required for someone to substantially shift the way they've been living. From a depth psychology perspective, we understand that there are periods in our lives that serve as catalysts for an initiation into the next developmental stage of who we are becoming.

As we've previously noted, today's thresholds of initiation are often catalyzed by a death, a divorce, a diagnosis, or a prolonged period of internal angst that can longer be tolerated. These moments become like a jolt to the psyche—a profound reminder that our time in these bodies is sacred, limited, and not to be taken for granted. When we zoom out on the cultural context of what we're programmed to believe a good life should consist of, the disruption of unconscious life patterns that a midlife crisis consists of could conceivably be more appropriately described as a midlife awakening. Of course, it doesn't often feel that simple to those left in the riptide of this type of pattern interruption. One person's awakening can be experienced by others as abandonment, betrayal, or the stimulus for what feels like insurmountable grief.

Instead of continuing to perpetuate the narrative that a midlife shift of consciousness should be viewed as a shame-filled breach of sanity occurring for those who dare to step outside of the normative cultural order, what I think can be a useful exercise would be to get curious about what was being suppressed within this individual up to this point—the origin points of their suppression, and how this form of suppression creates ripples of harm to the fundamental aspects of who we, as a society, are.

I often speak about how my time working as a couples therapist has convinced me that there's an unspoken war of the sexes being played out in our relationships, one which very few people seem to be curious about or eager to see come to an end. The funny thing about the art of war, and how I see it playing out so frequently between men and women, is that it's often a battle for control of one another's life force energy. It's a covert game of manipulation, distancing, domination, score-keeping, reactivity, and mistrust. It's what happens when we attempt to bring a wounded masculine framework to the art of loving. And it's incredibly confusing to our psyches, because we begin to experience an inner battle between the part of us that longs to embody our feminine qualities (authentic connection, trust in life, going with the flow, openhearted receptivity) and the ways that our rational minds have been conditioned to view every feminine aspect of who we are with a general sense of mistrust and contempt.

Here's an example of what I mean. I was having a conversation with a friend one day (who coincidentally also works in the realm of couples work and examining our relationship to love and partnership) and we were talking about the phenomenon of couples competing for control of one another's life force energy. She shared with me that when she first met her partner, before she'd started to do some of her own healing work, she'd found his career path as a touring musician to be threatening.

She recalled through an embarrassed grimace on her face, "I think I even had the conscious thought, 'How am I going to "tame" that out of him?'" I smiled in deep recognition of ways I had shown up similarly in the relationships of my past. I smiled because this is one small example of the countless ways we are conditioned to use domination as a way to minimize another human being's life force in an attempt to make our wounded ego mind feel safe.

And this type of covert domination is in no way exclusive to the ways that women attempt to assert control over another person once they've joined together in a relationship. In his book *Born a Crime*, Trevor Noah describes his mother's explanation of this energetic dance between men and women: "The way my mother always explained it, the traditional man wants a woman to be subservient, but he never falls in love with subservient women. He's attracted to independent women. 'He's like an exotic bird collector,' she said. He only wants a woman who is free because his dream is to put her in a cage."[5] The societal rationale for executing this form of dominance is that a woman who "respects" her man will minimize her sensuality, her freedom of expression, her playfulness, and the trust in her own intuitive urges—all in exchange for the safety she will experience within the containment of a relationship. In reality, there is an unconscious confrontation of a man's distorted relationship to the feminine that is never acknowledged when his immediate response is to control the feminine essence of the woman he's in a relationship with.

Regardless of which gender is being molded into a more "suitable" version of themselves to fit into the constructs of what society has deemed should make their partner feel safe, if we don't confront the fears that are being suppressed, they will inevitably come to the surface in some less than desirable ways. In his memoir titled *Memories, Dreams, Reflections*, Carl Jung wrote, "I have frequently seen people become neurotic when they content themselves with inadequate or wrong answers to the questions of life. They seek position, marriage, reputation, outward success of money, and remain unhappy. Even when they have attained what they were seeking. Such people are usually confined within too narrow a spiritual horizon. Their life has not sufficient content, sufficient meaning. If they are enabled to develop into more spacious personalities, the neurosis generally disappears."[6]

The truth is, what society has coded as a mental breakdown, lashing out, or someone going through a midlife crisis is the reality of what happens within the human psyche when we attempt to suppress aspects of who we are. The illusion of safety cultivated within a wounded masculine paradigm of control and domination leads to the emergence of the suppressed feminine in what might be classified as some maladaptive ways. This often looks like infidelity, reckless spending, extreme conflict, or emotional shutdown. Once these issues arise, those in relationship with the person who's reached their breaking point understandably focus on the hurt, confusion, and betrayal they feel in the aftermath of their sense of security being shattered. But rarely do we encourage an archaeological dig into the origin points of what has just occurred. We normalize relationships that lack the authentic experience of intimacy and where our insecurities and pain points drive us to assert our will over another, and call that loving. But the feminine energetics of who we are will not be suppressed forever; the Feminine will make her way to the surface eventually, and (sometimes) leave a wake of destruction in her path.

CHAPTER 6

A Toolkit to Bring You Back Home

"only if you find peace within yourself, will you
find true connection with others."

PALM READER, *BEFORE SUNRISE*

You Were Never Broken

when we come to the realization that a particular way of being is no longer
serving us—addictive tendencies, self-abandoning behaviors, minimizing our potential, or consistently struggling to experience peace in our
skin—there's a tendency to feel untethered and hopeless. Until we find
an alternative option. In other words, in order to interrupt detrimental
patterns that we've been using as our survival strategy, we need to replace
them with a new way of being. But before we can release a pattern to
make space for the next iteration of who we are meant to become, it
becomes really important to honor the place this survival strategy held
in our lives while it was here. Even our most unfavorable patterns have
served as tools to keep us afloat, until we realize one day that we are
starting to drown.

Patriarchal healing modalities put an emphasis on the idea that we
are somehow broken or abnormal, and that recovering from our abnor-
mality looks like finding our way back to living in accordance with the
societal status quo. And while this wounded masculine framework may
help us secure our need for belonging and the assurance of knowing
that our suffering will not cause us to be ostracized, it does very little
to question the core wound that was driving these survival strategies to

begin with. Our current healing models are lacking in the who, what, where, when, why, and how investigatory work that helps us to solve any mystery. If there's a dependency on drugs and alcohol, *what* feeling did those substances offer you that felt inaccessible for you to feel on your own? If you're continuously ending up in partnerships where you feel a sense of rejection, *where* did you learn the core beliefs about your innate self-worth? If you're struggling with anxiety or depression, *how* did your foundational experiences leave you feeling a fundamental lack of safety in your skin?

Until recently, Western approaches to healing have focused on mitigating the symptoms that present externally. This is a masculine treatment model. The masculine—even anatomically—creates with an external focus. The masculine is linear energy. Problem to solution. Pain to relief. Symptom to suppression of symptom. A linear approach isn't concerned with the deeper inquiry of who, what, where, when, why, and how. This is why there is such a hefty focus on pharmaceutical resolutions in a patriarchal culture. A wounded masculine approach holds that our singular focus should be on eliminating the symptoms as quickly as possible—without a great deal of inquiry around *what* was at the root of the symptom.

A feminine approach to healing, however, is primarily focused on the exploration. This investigation invites a curiosity about the original pain point that initiated the thing that we are grappling with. As we move the objective of healing away from fixing toward an effort to understand, we experience a tremendous amount of respite within our psyche. It gives us permission to put down the boulder we've been carrying—believing that we are somehow broken, defective, or different from everyone else—and begin questioning when, where, why, and how in the world we first got the idea that being like everyone else should be our goal. It's the starting point for one of my absolute favorite therapeutic inquiries: what else could be true?

I don't think I felt safe to honestly ask the question "What else could be true?" until my marriage ended. Up to that point, my sole focus had been on maintaining the attachment to my external sources of safety. I carried the belief that someone or something outside of me knew the best course of action for my life. It never really occurred to me that a sense of safety could be derived within myself. And listen—for years, I thought I had initiated the process of finding safety within. Mostly when I learned to stay present with myself through the turbulence that comes to the surface when we stop using drugs and alcohol. But without the complete dissemination of the other release valves I was using to avoid pain, I got stuck there.

We use all of our various vices and indulgences as a way to avoid being present with ourselves. And relationships can be one of the most comfortable places we as human animals have been trained to hide out. We are taught to distract ourselves from our own stages of evolution by focusing on what the person we are in a relationship with is or isn't doing right, how they feel about us, who else they might be giving their time or energy to, and whether or not the relationship will stand the test of time. While we're consumed with this barrage of thoughts about the external entity known as our partner, we're completely distracted from the things we'd rather not confront within.

When my relationship ended, I was forced to sit with myself in a conscious way for the first time in—I want to say fourteen years, but who am I kidding? It was the first time in my whole life that I'd really been forced to sit alone in the fire of my own solitude. No distractions. No one to save me. No release valve of numbing with drugs or alcohol. Just me, and a solemn invitation to get reacquainted with my true self for the very first time.

And here's what I learned: **there was never anything wrong with me**. After all those years believing that I was difficult to love, fundamentally broken, easily overwhelmed by emotions, and would never truly experience peace in my skin, I realized I'd just been waiting a lifetime to come home to that sacred inquiry of "What else could be true?" Understanding how to honor my Soul enough to care about the truth of how things felt was the secret sauce required to alleviate suffering.

This inquiry is the return to the hallowed darkness of our inner feminine. The retrieval of our own shadow—the wild untamable truths, the mystery that births within obscurity, the ecstatic dance between ever-shifting sensations, the vast complexity of the unknown, and the rich perception of our aliveness. Any form of polarization that leans too far in one direction will create an imbalance. The societal emphasis on masculine structures providing us with the perception of safety has left us with a collective deficit in our experience of feminine aliveness. And that aliveness means *all* of what being fully alive entails: the grief *and* the excitement, the discipline *and* the pleasure, the torture *and* the celebration, the rage *and* the compassion, the grounding *and* the exploration, the heartbreak *and* the eros. We came into these bodies to feel it all.

But feeling it all can be absolutely terrifying after a lifetime of being told that there are some sensations it's not safe to feel. We need methods of supporting our nervous system as it comes into the awareness that all of our emotions are safe to be felt and processed. This is how we integrate the understanding that we are both physical and spiritual beings. We learn to stay in our bodies through emotional waves as they move through us, while reminding ourselves that these waves are not the larger truth of who we are. This isn't an awareness that can be grasped on an intellectual level. Similar to the visceral sense of resilience that comes after someone stands up on a surfboard and rides a wave for the first time, our nervous system has to feel the sensation of resilience that comes from riding the waves of difficult emotions and coming out on the other side. There are countless ways to find our way back home to ourselves. For each of us, some of the most vital work we will do in this lifetime is developing our own toolkit for returning home to ourselves—a toolkit that feels true and right to our Soul. At this point, my toolkit feels pretty solidified. Of course, I will always be open to and in the space of gathering up additional tools. But I want to share some of the ones that have had the most profound impact on my journey up to this point.

The "How" Of Taking Your Power Back

Tool #1: Come Back into Your Body

I went to my first yoga class in my mid-twenties at a gym. I had been an avid runner for years—mostly with a punitive mindset and an attempt to control my weight. One day, after several weeks of pushing through what I could feel was a budding injury, my ankle reached a breaking point and I was unable to run a single step. At this point, skipping a day of working out didn't feel like an option for me. I climbed off the treadmill and decided to see what other group fitness classes I might be able to jump into. I remember being exceedingly irritated to see that the only thing available for the next several hours was a yoga class. But I felt desperate to do *something* to work up a sweat, so I decided to give it a try.

The class was every bit as irritating as I'd expected it to be. The teacher was unnecessarily cheerful, the poses were slow and intentional, and the meditative background music was the exact opposite of the motivational hip-hop I usually used to push through my runs. But at the end of the class the teacher asked us to lie down on our mats, extend our arms and legs, and completely release into a few minutes of stillness for something she called savasana (or corpse pose). At first I felt overwhelmed with agitation—like someone was constraining me in a situation that I desperately wanted to get out of. I'd never experienced anything like this before and it felt absolutely ridiculous. I didn't want to make a scene by getting up and leaving a quiet, dark room full of people, so I decided to close my eyes and try to relax. All of a sudden, the strangest sensations started to come over me. I felt a swell of emotions come to the surface. Suddenly I was crying—and not the small tear streaming down my cheek type of cry—no, this was the buckets of tears, "ugly cry" type of cry that Oprah often talks about. I hadn't even thought about anything sad at all. It was like something about being in that state of stillness forced my nervous system into the cathartic release of emotions I hadn't even realized I was holding. At the time, I didn't understand what was happening. But for some reason, I was intrigued and needed to know more.

Almost immediately following that first class, I became obsessed with the exploration of yoga. After I went to every different type of yoga class offered by my gym, I decided to expand my exploration to yoga studios all over town—power yoga, ashtanga, Iyengar, Kundalini, Bikram, yin/restorative yoga, and vinyasa flow. I realized that there was something in each of the various styles of yoga that not only challenged me in ways that I found incredibly inspiring, but also that something about it was changing my relationship with myself. This practice was building a confidence in me that I couldn't yet understand. This world of yoga—these studios, these poses, these sweaty practices with just me and a 24x70-inch piece of vinyl rubber—all of it was becoming like my own little secret love affair. I could feel myself getting stronger in ways that had nothing to do with the aesthetics of how I looked to the outside world. Witnessing my own progression from being unable execute a pose to feeling powerful as I used my breath to effortlessly move into the same pose a few months later made me feel proud of myself in the most authentic way.

My relationship with yoga continued to evolve over the years. It became the one constant in my life through the turbulence of my life's other growing pains. My yoga mat became my sanctuary—no matter where I was, or what I was going through, yoga was my means of remembering that (just as is true of the yoga poses we explore on the mat) no state of being is ever permanent. As my practice continued to progress, I eventually felt a pull to share what I was learning. The various yoga teacher trainings I took part in taught me about the science behind this yoga. I learned about the connection between our mind, our body, and our Spirit. And that while Western culture and ways of being teach us to place a particular emphasis on the mind and the external (an emphasis on the masculine), Eastern practices teach us to get out of the head and back into the sensations of the body—with the intention of returning to an awareness of our Spirit (an emphasis on the feminine).

While yoga was the jump-off point for me, the various modalities I've used over the years to experience embodied connection have fluctuated. I've learned that different seasons of life call for different resources for finding embodiment. Whether it's somatic dance, weight training, going for a walk, or diving into the ocean, I often tell clients it's less about *how* you get into your body, than it is about carving out some time and space to be present and allow our bodies to bring forward and release what needs to felt. In more recent years, I've found my way back to a relationship with running, but this time, with a completely different intention and ability to stay present with my body as it runs. Running has become a ritual of appreciation instead of deprivation. These days I find myself having an emotional release after a long, meditative run in the same way I did at the end of my first yoga class so many years ago. Our bodies continue to store the emotional remnants of what our rational mind makes every attempt to suppress. As Bessel van der Kolk rightly points out in *The Body Keeps the Score: Brain, Mind, and Body in the Healing of Trauma*, "No matter how much insight and understanding we develop, the rational brain is basically impotent to talk the emotional brain out of its own reality."[1]

So many of us have been conditioned to live in our bodies from the neck up. We've been taught to believe that we can rationalize our way through our human experience. But we can no more sever ourselves from our connection to our bodies without consequence than we can sever ourselves from the sensory experience of the feminine essence that these bodies represent. When we attempt to discount the very real experiences of pain that our lives generate within our psyche, conditions like anxiety, depression, addictions, chronic pain, and diseases show up in the body as psyche's way of saying to us, "There are feelings here to be felt. I will not allow you to ignore me." Coming back into relationship with our bodies becomes the first step in reclaiming our relationship with the inner feminine we were programmed to reject early on.

Tool #2: Meditate

Yoga Chitta Vritti Nirodhah was a phrase I was taught when learning about Hindu philosophy and the ancient language of Hinduism called Sanskrit during one of my first yoga teacher trainings. At the time, I understood this phrase to be suggesting that the purpose of yoga—and ultimately the larger practice of mediation that the asana or physical practice of yoga is one branch of—was the work of learning to "quiet the fluctuations of the mind in order to achieve self-realization." I have since come to a different interpretation of the larger meaning of this phrase. In Sanskrit, this phrase breaks down to:

Yoga—to join or unite

Chitta—consciousness

Vritti—fluctuations

Nirodhah—to quiet

Because I now believe that self-realization is not a state that any of us fully achieve while we are still living in these bodies, I see this phrase as describing the ongoing practice of consciously observing the fluctuations of our minds so that we may experience a bit more peace throughout our day. I'm sharing this because I think this is the most common misconception we have about cultivating a meditation practice. We have a tendency to believe that the objective of meditation is to sit in stillness and quiet our minds. This can make us believe that we aren't very good at meditating when we sit down and attempt to shut off our thoughts. But the mind, by its very nature, will never be quiet. It will continue to bring incessant thoughts to the surface because that is the precise thing the mind was designed to do. Instead of seeing meditation as an attempt to quiet the fluctuations of the mind, if we see it as the practice of being in conscious observation of the thoughts that come to the surface, we have an opportunity to be *in relationship* with our thoughts. We can observe, challenge, and be inspired by the thoughts that arise when we finally give ourselves permission to be still.

I heard someone say once, "Prayer is how we speak to the Divine. Meditation is how the Divine speaks back to us." Meditation is how we come into presence long enough to reconnect to our relationship with the Source energy that lives within. I don't believe there's a right or wrong way to meditate any more than I believe there's a right way or wrong way to be in relationship with a Higher Power of your own understanding. I've heard of people cultivating meditation practices while hiking in nature, riding waves on their surfboards, dancing at a concert with thousands of people, developing a mindfulness practice in traffic, or running around a playground with a small child. The point of meditation is to find a method of consciously observing the voice of the ego long enough to make space to connect to the voice of our Soul. Because the ego will always speak first, and the ego will always speak loudest. Meditation is our means of accessing the still, small voice within that sounds like the voice of love.

Tool #3: We Heal in Community

In Laura McKowen's memoir *We Are the Luckiest: The Surprising Magic of a Sober Life*, she offers a detailed account of her journey to sobriety. I was so moved by the refreshing level of vulnerability and candor McKowen offers in the pages of her memoir, but I felt a particular form of resonance while reading a chapter she titled, "Find a House Where the Truth is Told."[2] Anyone who's ever participated in any sort of twelve-step community or recovery work will tell you, there's something that feels slightly jarring to our nervous system when confronted with the level of transparency shared in these rooms, after a lifetime of being conditioned to lie to ourselves and others in one form or another.

And when I say conditioned to lie, I'm talking about the skeletons we're taught should never be allowed to exit our closets. The parts of ourselves we believe are too shameful for anyone to possibly know about and still see us as worthy of love. These are the despicable, harmful, rock-bottom moments of our lived experience that most people imagine you can't return from, let alone speak about out loud in front of a room full of strangers. These are the truths told in these healing communities in a way that suddenly makes you see that the parts of yourself you believed were most broken are the parts that make you most relatable to someone who's been feeling the same way about themselves.

My perspective on twelve-step groups is not easily boiled down to a black-and-white opinion—especially in the midst of a larger conversation about how we've been impacted by a wounded patriarchal culture. Aspects of these groups hold wounded patriarchal values in ways that it can be challenging to overlook. For instance, suggesting that some of us are inherently broken, while there are those among us who can use alcohol and drugs "normally"; a shame-based system of starting your days in recovery back at zero after a relapse of any kind; the suggestion that you label yourself as an addict or alcoholic forever; and identifying with what are described as your "character defects" are among some of the critiques I've heard voiced about twelve-step communities. And honestly, while many of these critiques are fair, in my opinion, they do not cancel out the larger value these programs offer.

Because for many of us, twelve-step rooms were our first exposure to the concept of being vigorously honest, a useful toolkit of helpful expressions and solutions, and a group of people suggesting that they have the capacity to hold love for us until we can learn how to love ourselves. For many of us, this type of fellowship offers the first experience of authentic belonging that we had no idea we'd been waiting a lifetime to feel.

I've heard members of various Indigenous communities speak about the ways they usher a new baby into the community upon arrival. There is often a belief that the most important thing a community can possibly express to a child is, "You belong with us." These communities remember what our modern society often fails to understand; from the moment we come into these human bodies, we feel a low-grade existential angst—a desire to feel that our presence here matters. Our culture teaches us that we need to hustle for the experience of unconditional acceptance through achievement, status, notoriety, or fame. This is what I often describe as a capitalist society that weaponizes our fundamental human need to feel that we belong. We're taught that we will be worthy once we've *earned* that worth instead of understanding that we come into our lives worthy—that worthiness is our innate birthright.

This is our indoctrination into the abandonment of our feminine. This is the establishment of the misconception we are sold—that we are no more than what we are able to accomplish during our time spent in these bodies. I will always hold with sacred reverence the rooms of the twelve-step communities, because although I no longer hold the belief that I'm any more of an addict than anyone else, these rooms helped me shed the deeply held limiting beliefs about my perceived difference. They taught me that you can speak your biggest, scariest fears out loud to a room full of people and the sun will come up again the next morning. They taught me that service and being accountable to something or someone larger than yourself is the clearest path to liberation. They taught me to get to know myself without filters, armor, or societal expectations. They taught me that there is sacred medicine in feeling like you belong. And that we can't know how desperate we've been to exhale into that belonging until it's the feeling we give ourselves permission to feel.

Tool #4: Radical Self-Forgiveness

There are certain constructs that a feminine perspective on healing asks us to let go of once and for all. A feminine viewpoint on what it means to heal is the returning to a Soul-based level of consciousness. Babies come into their bodies with this level of consciousness. None of us enter our lives with limiting ideations, the fear of failure or making a mistake, or believing that we are any more or less than the other humans around us—these are all the physical constraints of the ego mind that must be taught. Patriarchal religious ideologies that point to concepts of "good" and "evil" offer retributory constructs as the explanation for what we're meant to be doing with the lives we've been given, and what happens to us after we die. They propose doctrine about "man's original sin" and a heaven we will experience in the afterlife. But this type of ideology begs the question: why would a benevolent God send us into these bodies with a tainted nature that we are meant to spend a lifetime making up for? And what is the point of coming here at all if the truest experiences of joy, freedom, aliveness, and abundance elude us until after we're dead? This is an extremely fear-based conceptualization of life and further evidence of the desire for dominance that existed within the wounded masculine paradigms that constructed it.

The existence of free will means that each of us get to decide for ourselves which larger versions of Truth we find resonant. But in order to determine what is resonant or not, we have to ask ourselves if the beliefs we are believing are bringing us closer to a sense of peace, or if they are contributing to our experience of suffering. I once heard Reverend Michael Beckwith describe, during a Sunday service, the main difference between religion and spirituality in this way:

- religions attempt to tell you what you are meant to think about life

- spirituality offers you a set of tools for you to think about life for yourself

Søren Kierkegaard said, "Life can only be understood backward, but it must be lived forwards."[3] The beautiful thing about aging is seeing that so many of the moments in life filled with turmoil and isolation—the missteps and blunders, the seasons of feeling lost and out of control—inevitably shift and are transmuted into something that offers us a deeper sense of meaning. This is how we come to understand this life in the larger framework of a journey. Retrospection allows us to see the grace that is woven through each difficult period, helping us learn what we were ultimately meant to understand.

The feminine interpretation of life positions our experience in the context of the Soul. The Soul is the part of us that is eternal and conscious of the essence of love that resides within each of us. The Soul does not judge our actions as right or wrong, good or bad, but rather in or out of alignment with the essence of love that we are. And when we step out of alignment with love (as we inevitably will, as a necessary variable of what it means to be human), the suffering that we experience from the perspective of the ego is the result of our misalignment with the larger truth of who we are. But these moments of misalignment become our life's greatest teachings. Experiencing the contrast between what is out of alignment with our truth and what is in alignment with what we believe can only be solidified through the process of being in misalignment.

It's kind of like when someone tells a child who's never experienced a hot stove not to touch it because they could be hurt. If that child has no concept of what it feels like to be burned, they may need the experience of that particular brand of pain to have the understanding of a hot stove solidified within their psyche. The feminine perspective on this process of trial and error is understanding our times spent in these bodies as a continual process of expansion. We are meant to have moments where we get burned, to create the clarity within us about what kind of life we want to live. Just as it would be incredibly cruel to punish that child who touched a stove, demeaning them for making a mistake and getting something wrong that they didn't understand, it is incredibly short-sighted in the larger context of our life's continual expansion process to demean ourselves (or others) for stumbling along our path. How else could we learn?

The practice of radical self-forgiveness is a practice of acceptance. It acknowledges the futile nature of dwelling on a yesterday we are completely incapable of doing anything about. It recognizes our own innate power to build a future that is limitless by letting go of the suffering that results from the idea that the past can be anything other than what it was. We're often attempting to hold ourselves accountable for the things we did before we had the insight that the present moment offers us. But we didn't come here to do this life perfectly; we came into this life to expand.

Tool #5: Let Spirit Take the Lead

There has been a great deal of debate about whether or not Albert Einstein once said, "There are only two ways to live your life. One is as though nothing is a miracle. The other is as though everything is a miracle." I have always loved this quote, and whether or not these words can be accurately attributed to Einstein, the premise of this statement becomes an extremely personal conclusion that each of us must come to for ourselves. And while I have come to understand that the second half of this statement is an accurate interpretation of the nature of reality, I have neither the ability nor the interest in attempting to convince anyone of something that doesn't feel true to them. When I speak to others about my spiritual perspectives these days, I usually say that these are my interpretations of the teachings and spiritual concepts I've gathered up to this point. But they are just that, *my perspectives*, and I think each of us have to come to our own understanding about what ultimately feels true. What I will say that I know for sure to be true is that the more I believe in wonder, possibility, Divine timing, and a natural order and rhythm to the unfolding of life, the more life demonstrates to me the extent to which that is the precise nature of reality.

Most of us were raised with an understanding of God, Spirit, the Universe, Allah, Holy Spirit, Bhagavan, the Divine, or whatever name we correlated with a power greater than ourselves, as an external entity or authority figure. What I have come to understand over time is that just like a cup of ocean water that is drawn from the ocean is still the ocean (even as it takes on the physical form of water in a cup), we are not separate from the miraculous entity from which we originated. That cup of ocean water carries the same physical properties as its source. If and when it returns to the ocean, it will flow back into the realization of its original form. The same is true of each and every one of us. We are each unique emanations of God, Spirit, the Universe, Allah, Holy Spirit, Bhagavan, the Divine, or whatever name we correlate with a power greater than ourselves—embodying a human form for a brief period of time.

What this shift in consciousness brings into our awareness is that if each of us are no more—but certainly no less—than the eternal entity from which we originated, so is every single human being we meet. American theologian and author Marianne Williamson often references the spiritual text *A Course in Miracles* as saying, "All of the children of God are special, and none of the children of God are special."[4] Each of us are like little cups of the ocean, operating under the illusion that we are an individual cup of water. This is what some spiritual teachers refer to as the *original separation wound*. It's the false belief we carry that we are separate from unconditional love. In psychological terms, this is sometimes referred to as a *narcissistic wound*. But clinical psychology refers to this wound as the realization that we are separate from the unconditional love of our human caregivers. In reality, the larger pain point is carrying the false belief that we are separate from the energy that created us. Carrying this belief is painful because on a Soul level, we are aware that this misunderstanding of what we are ultimately holds us back from the work we came into these bodies to do. It's like moving through our lives with a sort of amnesia about who we are and what we are capable of. The deeper part of us that remembers that we are made up of the entity that created the entire Universe desperately longs for us to wake up and remember the capital-T Truth of who we are. This is a shift in consciousness from identification with ego to identification with Soul.

But here's the good news. The process of remembrance is a large part of what we came here for. So often, the Soul work that each of us is uniquely qualified for is based on the understandings we've gained from the experiences we have throughout our lives. Meaning, if we didn't have the precise relationships, pain points, missteps, growing edges, heartbreaks, and light-bulb moments of our specific life experience (unfolding exactly as they unfold), we wouldn't be as uniquely qualified to show up in the world and support the larger expansion of the human race as only we can.

This can be an extremely tough pill for our ego mind to swallow. Our ego will protest and rail against this understanding by questioning, "Why would a benevolent God or even the larger God Self that exists within me purposely create situations that would cause me to suffer?" The answer is that very rarely are we moved into the space of profound action when we feel comfortable. It's the adversity that creates passion, cultivates break-throughs, and ultimately generates a desire within us to understand.

Once we shift from ego consciousness to Soul consciousness, we are more willing to view everything that comes up in our lives through the larger context of how we are being expanded. And this is not just through moments of adversity; we experience an immense amount of expansion through moments of pleasure, grace, fulfillment, and joy. But the ego mind resists life-affirming moments as well. So often when we're experiencing expansion through blissful moments, the ego will be skeptical and avoid being present—certain that at any moment the other shoe will drop.

On the flip side, in moments of difficulty, the ego will contract, identifying these moments as evidence that life is incredibly unfair. But the larger truth that our Soul is aware of is that life is neither fair or unfair. All of the suffering that our ego mind encounters is based on the story we're telling ourselves about what our lives should or shouldn't be. But when we bring ourselves back to a larger state of awareness—that we are something much larger than our pain points—we start to shift our consciousness back into the space of inquiry.

And so, what is the tangible tool for the moments when we feel hijacked by the overwhelming fears of the ego? I always think about something I heard Dr. Wayne Dyer say in a talk years ago. I knew in my bones that this phrase would be a game changer the moment I heard it. He said something like: the mantra of the lower self is, "I need more." The mantra of the higher self is, "How do I serve?" The ego mind will *always* find a reason that it needs more of something: certainty, validation, comfort, recognition, control, resources, you name it. The Soul remembers that we are little cups of God—and if God (or whatever resonant name we use to describe a higher power) *is* love, we already have existing within us every single thing we could possibly ever need. Our cup is running over with nothing but love to give. And from that full cup, we're able to let go of the false belief that we need anything outside of ourselves to be whole. This practice brings us back to the conscious awareness that we are the embodiment of the loving energy that created everything that surrounds us. And from this awareness, not only does our life begin to feel a bit more miraculous, but we are suddenly in the imaginal space of unlimited possibility.

None of This Is Random

When I first moved to LA in 2007, I could feel an expansion happening in the collective recognition of ourselves as spiritual beings having a temporary human experience. I saw that more and more people were prioritizing self-inquiry over disassociation and partying. Conversations around spirituality, self-actualization, presence, and healing were becoming more and more commonplace. I had been immersed in the world of yoga for a few years by the time I arrived, and I was eager to find and practice with some of the yoga teachers who had brought an awareness of this practice to the mainstream. It didn't take a great deal of research to realize that Exhale Center for Sacred Movement in Venice was the studio that housed some of the most potent voices in the yoga community at the time. Shiva Rea, Saul David Raye, and Seane Corn were just a few of the resident teachers making this little space in the world feel like the Mecca for any and all who had the desire to deepen their relationship with this sacred practice.

I'm mentioning this studio and these teachers by name because a fundamental aspect of yoga philosophy is to pay homage to the lineage of teachers who helped you understand what you have come to know. These teachers not only supported me in healing some of the distorted ways I'd learned to be in relationship with my body, but also opened my mind to new ways of exploring the concept of God and what it means to be spiritual. I started referring to this studio as my yoga church—and not because the classes were filled with dogma and attempts to proselytize students into a certain way of thinking, but because each class felt like a solemn invitation to the world of spiritual inquiry.

I remember one day in class, I heard Saul David Raye say, "To define God is to deny God." For some reason, these words hit me like a ton of bricks. And still, I didn't realize the enormity of what he was saying at the time. I didn't understand that he was speaking about the vast complexity of the omnipresent feminine essence that is synonymous with Source energy. And that any attempt to label, compartmentalize, minimize, or truly understand the energetic that is responsible for all of creation (the feminine) is a laughable endeavor to say the very least. It's not so much that we shouldn't explore the nature of exactly what this essence is, but rather that *as* we question we are meant to be in a state of awestruck wonder, reverence, and acceptance that there are aspects of the Universe that will always be beyond our human capability to fully grasp.

This fact can feel simultaneously terrifying and thrilling, depending on where we are on the continuation with our relationship to trust. And this relationship, as with all relationships, is not meant to be a static one. In some moments our ability to trust in the perfect nature of the unfolding Universe is more accessible to us than at others. This is the nature of what it means to be in the continuous dance between the fears that arise from our ego mind and the practice of returning to the knowing that exists within the depths of our Soul.

But, if and when we inhabit the Soul space more often than we allow our lives to be dictated by fear, we start to receive little nudges from the Universe as indications that we are held and cared for by a force larger than ourselves. We realize that we are meant to live with far more freedom than the world around us might suggest, and that concepts like fate and destiny are crucial elements of the Soul's larger purpose for us coming into these bodies. There's an important distinction to be made between fate and destiny. Fate has to do with the people, experiences, and opportunities that were predetermined to be a part of our life story. Destiny is the decision we make (or choose not to make) to keep moving toward our life's highest potential. Destiny is not synonymous with the suggestion that the lives we are living are anything other than our own. Each of us comes into this life fated to experience our own gifts, pain points, and moments of growth, all of which have the potential to play a part in what our Soul understood to be life's curriculum, pointing us toward our destiny long before we came here.

This recognition becomes the establishment of a Soul-centered life. Our ego will attempt to reject the elements of fate that feel out of alignment with the limited perspective it holds about what our lives "should" be. But our ego is often shortsighted in this attempt to muscle its way into the circumstances of its restrictive agenda. Our Soul's perspective is vast and creative, abundant and unafraid. The Soul carries the understanding of the highest Truths of who we are. The ego is usually making decisions from the space of its fear-based programming. And that's perfectly okay. Because our destiny doesn't have an expiration date. The time will never run out on our chance to step fully into the potential of what we came into our lives to accomplish. We may, however, cultivate a great deal more suffering for ourselves when we resist the components of fate that come into our lives to point us in the direction of our destiny.

We've been sold the lie that this life is something we are meant to struggle through. That if we're not in the constant state of resisting, attempting to know the future, worrying, and swimming against life's current, we'll never make our way downstream. It just isn't true. The resistance to *what is* creates the struggle. The lack of trust that we will persevere through any outcome creates what feels like unbearable suffering within our minds. And we have to offer ourselves so much grace around why this is the case. We live in a societal structure that celebrates consumerism, competition, workaholism, and a general belief in lack and limitation. This wounded masculine paradigm is the ego mind's playground. There's never a shortage of terrifying news cycles to reinforce the ego's belief that the world around us is fundamentally unsafe. There's always someone's social media highlight reel demonstrating the ego's assumption that everyone else is living a much more fulfilling life than we are. There's never a lack of things to buy, alcohol to consume, acknowledgment to chase, and agitation in the here and now for the ego to use as a distraction.

But within the Soul space, nothing is ever anything other than exactly as it's meant to be. Our Soul is not impatient with us, or judging our missteps, or feeling that life as we're living it is ever being wasted. Our Soul never forgets the destiny we came into this life school to experience, and it trusts in the path we choose to take. It's sort of like if you had a toddler in a padded, fenced in area with toys, learning tools, and games—all of which you were certain wouldn't hurt them. You would (hopefully) allow them to explore and learn and begin to understand what each tool in that padded area had to teach them. You wouldn't worry because you would know that they were in a safe space, experiencing what it is developmentally appropriate for them to understand. Even if they got frustrated with one of the puzzles, you'd understand that the puzzle was helping them learn. You'd feel compassion for their experience of frustration. But in the big picture, you'd know that this toddler was alright. That's how the Source energy that created us feels about us in this life school.

At the end of our lives, after we've played out our worldly dramas and grown through what we were meant to understand, we will return to the Source energy we were before we came into these bodies. Safe and sound. In Buddhist philosophy, this phenomenon is referred to as Maya. This is essentially the dream state each of us inhabits when we believe that the material world that surrounds us is real—or all there is. This is a sort of cosmic illusion, and what we awaken from when we come into the space of remembrance of who we really are.

Holding ourselves and our lives in the context of a "life school" set up to prepare us for the destiny we have the potential to experience is not a consistent state of consciousness for any of us. Maintaining that continuous awareness would be the equivalent of walking around in an embodied state of enlightenment. And if we were to come into these bodies fully aware of the highest Truth of who we are, what would we even be doing here? Returning to this state of remembrance was meant to be a lifelong practice. And just like yogis who get stronger and are changed by the poses they practice on a regular basis, we can certainly get stronger in our ability to hold the awareness that something larger is unfolding through the turbulent moments of our lives. But we will forget. And remember. And then forget again.

The universe supports us in this remembrance. Eventually we start to see life's synchronicities, chance encounters, humbling moments of enlightenment, and grace-filled nudges of inspiration as sacred signals that we are supported by something larger than our ego's limited perspective. The Source energy within each of us wants desperately for us to know that we are loved and supported. We just have to ask to be shown.

CHAPTER 7

The Dance of Eros

"the near enemy of love is attachment. attachment masquerades as love. it says, 'I will love this person (because I need something from them)' . . . true love allows, honors, and appreciates; attachment grasps, demands, needs, and aims to possess."

JACK KORNFIELD

What Happens When We Fall?

after my marriage ended, I began to see my work as a therapist through a different lens. I was humbled. I became a lot more curious about what I didn't understand. I felt a bit disillusioned by the promise of certainty and fulfillment that "happily ever after" narratives could ever really offer to any of us. From this state of disillusionment, something interesting started to happen. I noticed that (almost synchronistically) the majority of my client base began to be organized into two categories: couples who were struggling with their own relationship dissatisfaction, and singles (predominantly women) whose struggles seemed to be primarily centered around the reality of their singlehood. It was a fascinating juxtaposition between one group longing to be on the inside of a club that they felt their life circumstances had excluded them from, and those on the inside feeling disenchanted by the dream of love and partnership they'd once bought into. And as a single woman who'd spent 11.5 years on the "inside," I had a unique point of view as I sat with each population.

I found that certain themes came up with my clients so regularly, I started to expect them to be the topics we'd be processing each day.

With the single women, it was the feeling of their life's incompletion. They grappled with narratives around their lack of fundamental worthiness—wondering why they were never chosen, believing they were defective and sad, and that everyone around them had cracked a code they were simply unable to crack. This led to feelings of despair and hopelessness that, if I'm honest, I often felt inept at knowing how to support them through. I honestly didn't know if they would ever find the love and partnership they longed to experience. But I could see that their experiences of longing were impacting the emphasis they put on every single opportunity that came before them to experience love.

For instance, Meg was a single woman in her early forties. She had met all of the markers of conventional success—she'd gone to competitive schools, had thrived in several high-power jobs, and had successfully purchased the home of her dreams—but she spent the majority of our sessions working through the unbearable sense of sorrow she'd hidden away from the rest of the world. All of her success, everything she'd worked for, all of the symbols that would make her a desirable bachelor if she were a man, was (from her perspective) irrelevant in comparison to the gaping hole in her life created by her singlehood. Meg had a community of friends that seemed to adore her, she traveled all over the world for her work, and had the financial freedom to basically do anything at all that she wanted to do. But she couldn't buy a relationship. And that was the one goal she longed to accomplish far more than any of the others.

As Meg lamented the reality of her single status, she would often reflect out loud with a dumbfounded look on her face, "I just don't understand how I got here. I never imagined I'd be at this stage of life without anyone to share it with." When I asked Meg to give me an overview of what her relationships had looked like in the past, she described a series of entanglements with men that "didn't choose her." Chief among them was a seven-year relationship with Jason, who she described as "the workaholic guy from college." Jason had been determined not to let love and partnership derail what he wanted to accomplish in his career. What had made the demise of this particular relationship extremely painful was that shortly after he ended things with Meg, Jason had fallen hopelessly in love with someone else and immediately gotten married. Meg noted that she'd been stuck in the grief over her relationship with Jason for years. She'd had a series of affairs with married men at work; dated a few "lovely men" that she couldn't seem to find an authentic spark with, and then tried to settle into the acceptance that the marriage and children she'd desperately longed for just might not be in the cards for her.

Meg and I worked together for months, challenging the narrative that Jason's inability to choose her equated to her being fundamentally unlovable. We explored the possibility that sometimes people are meant to be in our lives for a season, and that when we resist seeing how a partnership isn't supporting our ability to honor and love ourselves well, the Universe will often remove that person from our lives in what can feel like a harsh way. This is meant to serve as a wake-up call, inviting us to choose ourselves a bit more fully. But if we stay in the resistance to seeing where that relationship was ultimately out of alignment, we can romanticize a dynamic as something other than what it truly was.

As Meg began to open up to seeing her history with Jason through a different lens, she eventually felt ready to dip her toes back into the dating pool. This new development in her life felt both thrilling and terrifying. I started to feel a bit protective of Meg as she demonstrated surges of euphoria from each direct message she received on her dating apps. We explored how she might use dating as an opportunity to meet some new people, without any attachment or expectation about where things might go. This idea was great in theory, but as anyone who's ventured into the Dating Wild West (also known as the world of dating apps) will tell you, it's a jungle in there. Perceived connections abruptly ending when someone loses interest—without any clarity or explanation; meeting someone for a date and finding that they look nothing at all like the pictures they've posted online; and feeling a sense of depletion with so many wrong fits to sift through before you can conceivably find a match are all commonplace occurrences in the modern dating world.

For Meg, I watched as each person she dated filled her with an initial swell of euphoria. She was experiencing bouts of hope and possibility as she fantasized about what their life together could become. But after a few dates and what seemed like a pattern of men pulling back their interest or ghosting her altogether, Meg's energy was completely deflated. It occurred to me that Meg's highs and lows were less about the actual person she was going out on dates with and more about the projected sense of self-worth she was placing upon each prospect. Meaning, when we are conditioned to believe that our self-worth lies in our ability to be chosen, each person we see as having the potential to choose us becomes the solution for our ego mind's perceived lack of wholeness. We begin to make this person responsible for healing our original separation wound. We project onto them the fantasy of being the key to our sense of fulfillment—essentially making them the connection to a Higher Power we've been seeking our whole lives.

This is another unspoken energetic transaction we make in dating. Incidentally, this is a fairly complex transaction we're attempting to negotiate with a complete stranger. "I will love you in exchange for you seeing me, adoring me, and filling me up in all the ways I've always longed to be seen, adored, and filled up for a lifetime." The trouble is, the other person's ego mind has its own fantasies of what romantic fulfillment would look like. And here's the important piece—their ideas are based on *their own* particular pain points and ways that *they* long to be seen, adored, and filled up. Sometimes, the energetic chemistry matches. Each person believes they've found the missing piece they've been longing to find. But more often than not, the desperate need of our energetic pull reminds that other person of something they'd rather not feel. We might make them feel overly needed in a way they despised as a child, or unseen in a way that reminds them of a particular parent. They might have a desire for something or someone who possesses completely different attributes than the ones we possess. Or sometimes, where that person is in their life is just not an energetic match for where we are.

The point is, the dance of energy between two people is a subconscious one, and a lot less personal than our ego mind attempts to make it when we feel rejected. Since the ego has decided that this person holds the key to our worthiness, when they decide to pull their energy back from us, the euphoric surge of energy we felt upon meeting is immediately drained, sending us back into the illusion of our lack of worthiness.

This energetic push and pull continues long after we enter into relationships. If and when we meet someone who we are initially on the same page with energetically (each person believing that the way they are being filled up is what they've been searching for), it becomes similar to the first ecstatic hit of the most amazing drug you can imagine. Falling in love floods our brain with dopamine and completely shifts our perception of the world around us. The colors seem a bit brighter, the daily annoyances of our lives seem to roll off our back with ease, and life is suddenly filled with possibility and wonder in a way that it hadn't been before this sacred Soul entered our life.

The trouble is, even when this person feels like an energetic match, they still have a lifetime of pain points that affect their ability to give and receive love. When each person's humanity starts to rear its inconvenient head (as it inevitably will), we start to feel like we're crashing down from that high. We feel shortchanged because this person is no longer filling us up with the energetic euphoria they used to, and a never-ending struggle ensues as we attempt to get that energy back.

Marco and Laurie were a perfect example of a couple who'd gone from a jubilant love affair to the resentment that ensues when we no longer provide one another with the same energetic high. The two of them had been together for five years. Each came into therapy ready to make their case for why this relationship was no longer meeting their needs. Marco felt strongly that Laurie's prioritization of work and female friendships made him feel like the least important thing in her life. Laurie argued that Marco's constant criticisms put her in the position of wanting to be anywhere else in the world but at home with him—most of the time. This adversarial stance is a very common dynamic within our romantic partnerships. We become so engulfed in our individual experiences of how our partner is no longer filling our lives with the assurance, support, and positive reinforcement that they offered when we first met that we feel shortchanged and often downright angry.

We feel this anger because our partner is no longer serving as the source of energetic replenishment that they once were. You've probably even heard people use phrases like, "This person doesn't fill my love cup anymore." But this phrase can (if we're willing) invite us to explore a larger existential question about the spiritual purpose of our partnerships. Meaning, if our Soul's work in this lifetime is to experience situations, pain points, and relationships that teach us specific lessons that bring us back into alignment with the highest version of who we are, is it really another person's responsibility to fill us up with a sense of wholeness if that's not how we authentically feel about ourselves? And what resources are they using to do that work for themselves, if they're constantly pouring into someone else's cup? But more importantly, even if they are able to pour their energy into our cup, filling us with the energetic assurance, support, and positive reinforcement that we desire, what happens to us when they can't? When they don't have the capacity, or feel depleted, or their life pulls them in a direction that is no longer in alignment with us?

Laurie expressed that Marco was consistently pointing out to her the ways she was falling short of loving him in the way that he longed to be loved. When she attempted to address his desire for more frequent sex, his response was that he'd like her to dress a bit sexier to get him in the mood. When she rushed home from work to have dinner together, he'd complain that having takeout didn't offer the quality time together that cooking a meal together would. Laurie found herself feeling more and more resentful that each time she attempted to hear and address one of Marco's needs, he'd move the goal post a bit further away. Marco felt insistent that when two people love each other, it meant doing whatever it takes to understand and meet their partner's needs. I wasn't so sure.

As I watched Marco and Laurie compete for who was the more incompetent in their ability to love the other well, I couldn't help but question: is this what it means for our Soul to love another Soul? To continuously point out their ineptitude at making us feel that we are worthy of their love? And if we're honest with ourselves, is that feeling of unworthiness really about our partner, or about the original separation wound that made us believe we were unworthy to begin with? Are we truly looking to love another person, or to fill the hole within us created by the caregivers and a society who didn't love and see us in the ways that we longed to be loved and seen? In other words, are we really looking for a partner—or are we looking for a parent?

When we allow the love we receive from another to serve as the validation that we are worthy of being poured into and cared for, our love cup becomes like a cup with a hole in the bottom—constantly needing to be filled, but never satiated. Because again, our Soul knows what our ego mind has forgotten: that we were never anything less than whole. But the wounded structures of the world around us convince us that we are incomplete. These wounded masculine structures teach us about protecting ourselves and winning at all costs; to live with an insatiable appetite for more, and to resist being present with what we have. We're taught to focus on what is lacking in all areas of our lives, instead of trusting in abundance. It's no surprise that everything this structure teaches us starts to bleed into our love lives as well. The suffering we experience in love comes from the part of us that knows that the way we've been taught to understand relationships has nothing to do with a relationship's true function.

Rejection Wounds

There's been a lot of attention centered on understanding attachment styles in the world of personal development recently. Many people have a pretty clear impression of what they believe is their primary attachment style. Although there is a complexity to what defines our way of experiencing safety in relationship to those around us, the nuance of British psychologist John Bowlby's original attachment theory seems to be lost in the collective understanding of people being either anxiously or avoidantly attached. In case you're not familiar with Bowlby's attachment theory, it explores our way of relating to others as a response to how securely attached we felt to our primary caretakers. While most of the emphasis has been placed on the anxious (insecure in attachments) and avoidant (fearful of attachments) attachment styles, there are several other variations on how attachment styles are expressed—and from my perspective, none of these attachment styles are fixed.

What is often lost in conversations about attachment styles is the recognition of humans as energetic beings. Because we pick up on the energetic frequency of everyone we come in contact with, so much of how safe or unsafe we feel in someone else's presence has to do with the energy they are emitting in any given moment. We often think of a secure attachment style as being the relational goal we're attempting to work toward, but I would argue that no one feels secure in their attachments all the time. Different relational dynamics, during different seasons of our lives and in different people's energy, will bring different relational wounds to the surface. The anxious energy we feel in one person's presence can completely shift when we're around someone whose energy creates a sense of relational safety.

One example of the irregular nature of these energetics that comes to mind is a client I worked with both before and after her divorce. In her marriage, Maggie had been playing out the role society teaches women to play in order to "catch" a man—nurturing and sweet, just sexy enough, thoughtful and pampering, and easy to get along with. But as we've previously discussed, the felt experience of everything society places within the job title of wife *and* mother often creates Academy Award-worthy actresses who eventually find themselves no longer interested in playing the role they've been cast in. So when a man at her office saw Maggie— not as the nurturing female persona she had been taught to present to a man in the hopes of being chosen, not as a wife and mother with a never-ending list of tasks that distracted her from being a separate Self, and not as an irritated, depleted, disconnected, resentful woman like the one she had started to see herself as—but really *saw her*, in her essence, complexity, and feminine radiance, she was completely caught off guard by realizing how hungry she'd felt to be seen. There was an innate feminine desire that had been lying dormant inside her for years.

While Maggie's relationship to love and partnership went through various phases after her marriage ended, regardless which of the phases Maggie was experiencing, there was one issue that seemed to consistently haunt her thoughts and immediately throw her into a tailspin—Rory. Rory and Maggie's affair had been what instigated the breakup between herself and her husband. Although Maggie had left her job while she was still married (a last-ditch attempt to convince her husband that everything between she and Rory had been a temporary lapse in sanity), the two of them still connected periodically and Maggie often referred to Rory as "her kryptonite."

When Maggie was a married woman, Rory seemed to find her irresistible. She would catch him gazing at her as though she was the most beautiful woman he'd ever laid eyes on; he would make thoughtful gestures like surprising her with her favorite muffin when he went on a coffee run; and when she finally gave into temptation and they started having an affair, he spoke of their connection as though it was unlike anything he'd experienced before. Maggie didn't tell me until long after their affair had ended that it was actually Rory pulling away from her that cemented her initial decision to come clean with her husband. Rory became like an obsession for Maggie. She found herself continuing to long for his attention, fantasizing about his touch, and dreaming of scenarios where the two of them would be on the same page again about their desires.

What's fascinating about the anxious attachment energy Maggie exhibited in her relationship with Rory is that it was the exact opposite of the energy she embodied in her relationship with her husband. In her marriage, Maggie was the avoidant one. She constantly felt like he was too needy, leaving her resentful of his persistent bids for connection. She even noted once that she finally felt like she understood how her husband had felt, demoralized by her desperate longing to be seen and connect with Rory. Each subset—Maggie and her husband, and then Maggie and Rory—are beautiful illustrations of how a pursuer/distancer dance plays out in relationships. Sometimes you'll hear people refer to this as a runner/chaser dynamic, or in the context of attachment styles— the dance between the anxious and the avoidant. The point is that as one person embodies one energetic end of a polarity, the other person instinctually responds accordingly. It's not conscious—it's intuitive.

So let's use the dynamic between Rory and Maggie as a means of unpacking the complex "why" underneath this energetic push and pull. When Maggie was unavailable to him, this placed Rory in the role of the pursuer, the hunter, the man on a mission. To a certain extent, *some* of this can be considered a form of healthy masculine energy. It was an energetic that made Maggie feel seen, desired, and receptive to a man in a way she hadn't felt in a very long time. An energetic shift started to happen between them, however, as Maggie felt a lack of containment from Rory. Containment meaning clarity around his intentions, the sense that he would be a stable and consistent force in her life, and enough self-awareness to move through their relationship dynamic with integrity and a sense of himself. Essentially, containment is synonymous with safety. This is one of the places that modern society attempts to shame women out of the realities of our biology. Casual sex can never feel exactly the same for a woman as it does for a man, because on a subconscious level, she has a primal response to the responsibility she would carry if she were to get pregnant with this man's child. She can instinctively sense when a man is not emotionally prepared to support her in this, and she starts to have a visceral response to this lack of safety.

A woman's response to the anxious energy this formulates within her normally looks like her taking over. She will attempt to bridge the gap between them—removing herself from the role of the receiver (her feminine energy) and taking on a leadership position (her masculine energy). She will pepper him with questions about his intentions, express her desire for more consistency, and attempt to create a sense of clarity between them for herself.

Now here's where the dance gets interesting. Rory (or the core masculine in this energetic scenario) can respond in one of two ways to the wounded masculine energy emitted by Maggie:

Option A: Rory could submit to this wounded polarity and begin to slowly embody the more wounded feminine energetic in their dynamic, the way that Maggie's husband had started to do in their marriage. Because this dynamic feels intrinsically unnatural to a core feminine—removing her from the essence that sparked her attraction to Rory to begin with—Maggie will eventually start to resent him, and feel turned off by Rory in the same way she was with her husband.

Option B: Rory could reject Maggie's invitation to formulate a wounded sense of polarity and withdraw into a wounded masculine energetic of his own—becoming cold and distant, emotionally cut off, and seemingly a bit narcissistic in his sudden unwillingness to see or care about how his actions were making her feel.

Because this is the option Rory chose, it immediately activated a sense of polarity in Maggie, sending her into a wounded feminine dynamic—chasing after Rory's love, insecure and desperate for his attention, and acting out in ways that were inauthentic to who she truly was.

This dance of polarities between the pursuer/distancer is such a common struggle in romantic relationships because we have been conditioned to misunderstand what intimacy looks like. We've made it the common practice to quickly respond to our physical attraction to one another before a foundation of emotional safety has been formed. This makes us feel extremely vulnerable and unsafe being authentic with one another.

I struggle with how often I hear women describe men like Rory as "fuck boys" or "narcissistic love bombers." One, because Rory's behavior *could* be argued as a natural response to the misaligned polarity that would have inevitably resulted in the demise of what magnetized he and Maggie to one another regardless. But also, putting all of the onus on Rory completely ignores the responsibility Maggie held in requiring a foundation of emotional intimacy with someone before becoming physically intimate. I don't actually think either of them is to *blame*, per se—and I don't necessarily carry the opinion that casual sex is a negative thing when two people are clear, boundaried, and certain that they're on the same page. But what I see more frequently being the case is that one person is withholding their *actual* feelings for the other—or stronger feelings develop over time that are not honestly expressed. This often results in one person longing to change the rules of the game halfway through.

The thing about the anxious and the avoidant attachment styles is that they both stem from a fundamental rejection wound experienced at the hand of a caretaker. They're essentially two sides of the same coin.

Anxious energy results when caregivers don't see and consistently tend to a child's needs. This causes a form of annihilation anxiety in a child, making them feel desperate for connection—fearing that without it, they'll be destroyed. Avoidant energy also results when caregivers don't see and tend to the needs of a child, but in the avoidant's case, the child internalizes the belief that they can't be seen, and shuts down their willingness to seek emotional intimacy. Both attachment injuries are caused by a wounded masculine energetic—a parent so consumed with their own narcissistic injury that they're unable to stay connected to their child—and both attachment styles are an invitation to honor the inner feminine that longs to be seen.

The beautiful thing about the seemingly impossible conundrum of dancing within these polarities (the pursuer/distancer dynamic, opposing attachment styles, or whatever we choose to call it) is that regardless of what the dynamic with another person is bringing forward, it serves as an invitation to bring the focus back home to ourselves.

Let's take Maggie for example. Both wounded relational polarities (with her husband and Rory) offered an opportunity for her to see how disconnected she had become from her authentic self. Her dynamic with her husband demonstrated that trusting in a societal template for her life instead of her own inevitably caused her to put on a wounded masculine armor. This made her feel resentful, cut off from her emotions, and quick to withdraw. She was given the opportunity to remember the depth of her own feminine essence when she met Rory. His unwillingness to join with her in the societal template Maggie had been conditioned to follow, however, activated wounded feminine attributes within her. She often noted that she didn't recognize the desperate, insecure, obsessive version of herself that Rory brought forward. It felt like a persona that took over her entire personality.

Attachment theory can be an incredibly useful tool for identifying the unprocessed pain that a relationship dynamic is mirroring back to us. Understanding our attachment style can become a hindrance, however, when we use it as a form of leverage to perpetuate our wounds. If Maggie would have dug her heels in on the fact that she was being victimized by

Rory, and that *his behavior* was responsible for the anxious energy within her, she'd miss the opportunity to see what his behavior was reflecting back to her about herself. She might miss the extent to which this relationship was shining a magnifying glass on her own shadow.

The shadow elements of our psyche, or the unconscious parts of who we are that we are resistant to seeing, will often show up when we feel triggered in our relationships. These activation points that come up with another person can be used as a tool for us to see ourselves a bit more clearly—and ultimately to come back home to ourselves. In truth, we're all just doing our best to love others within the framework of the pain points, wounds, and distorted lenses of conditioning we've been carrying from our life's experiences. When our rejection wounds inevitably come to the surface, the invitation becomes to see them as an opportunity to finally stop rejecting ourselves.

Ownership Templates

A spiritual perspective on partnerships suggests that each and every collision we have with another Soul happens because that person has come into our lives to demonstrate something that we are meant to learn at this juncture of our Soul's journey. It suggests that while people may come into our lives for a reason, a season, or (sometimes) the majority of our lifetime, regardless of the duration, each person we connect with has something to teach us about ourselves.

This is a radical departure from the understanding of partnerships that most of us grew up with. We're raised to believe that when the love of our life arrives, our lives will exponentially improve. This person will understand and comfort us in the way that no one else has before. We're taught that love means finding someone who sees and adores us, which allows us to finally exhale into the safety and containment we've always longed to feel. So much of this is really beautiful, and a great deal of what partnership *could* conceivably offer—if both people were to take wholehearted responsibility for their part in this energetic exchange. The trouble with this romantic premise is that it's a very externally focused vision of partnership. This person will *see me*. This person will *adore me*.

This person will be *in service of me*. But we're not taught to put a lot of emphasis on how to take responsibility for how we're showing up in relationship to this person.

A lot of this circles back to some of the previously named ownership templates of partnership that stem from our belief in a romantic love rooted in fairy tale ideologies. An ownership template suggests that once someone is *my* partner, *my* girlfriend, or *my* husband, there's a fair amount of behavioral compliance to be expected on this person's part. I start to have expectations of how this person will show up in an effort to be who I need them to be. We've been taught to believe that this is the purpose they are meant to serve in our lives. But if we hold that each individual Soul came into their body with specific lessons, fated moments, and a unique destiny that they have the potential to carry out, it becomes crucial to realize that it's never our place to feel a sense of ownership over another Soul. It doesn't matter how intimately connected we feel to them, how long we've been in a relationship, or how much we may long to hold onto them in the way that we desire. Each of us belongs to something bigger than these bodies, and that force is larger than any rule or restriction that our ego mind can construct.

Most of us have our first reckoning with this difficult truth in the moment we lose something we once believed would last forever. It wasn't until I was on the outside of my own marital structure that I was able to see clearly how misguided I was in the understanding that my husband was *mine* to own—or that I was ever his. I started to see that holding love this way causes us to take people for granted. We assume that we're entitled to having a partnership, when in reality, many people go an entire lifetime without experiencing one. This is the precise reckoning that one of my clients, Melissa, found herself contending with firsthand. Melissa, a single woman in her early thirties, had been a serial monogamist, going from one long-term relationship to another. And while she hadn't yet found the person who was the right fit for long-term partnership, she was feeling the ping of urgency that many women express in their early thirties as they watch their friends go through the process of engagements, followed by weddings, into the trajectory of the home and kids we've all been taught to consider the norm. We were in the midst of processing what this ping of urgency was bringing up for Melissa when Jacob entered her life.

The excitement Melissa felt as she was telling me about Jacob was palpable. He was thoughtful, charismatic, assertive but sweet, driven, and one of the best lovers Melissa had ever experienced being with. Right from the start, she described being certain of one thing—this was *her* husband. Things seemed to progress fairly smoothly in the beginning of their relationship. Melissa spent most of our sessions gushing about the time she spent with Jacob, how much her friends liked him, stressing about his previous relationships, fantasizing about their future together, and wondering when he might be ready to take things to the next level.

I often found myself interjecting, attempting to steer Melissa's focus back inward. Something about her pacing where Jacob was concerned felt a bit unnerving to me. It almost seemed frenetic. She suddenly seemed completely disinterested in any of the introspective work she had been doing, trading it for an all-consuming obsession with this budding romance. Of course, some of this is a natural response to falling in love. But something about how laser-focused Melissa's life had become (especially given that this laser focus was solely on decoding the intentions of another person) filled me with an intuitive sense of concern.

And then something happened eight months in that slowed Melissa's pace down to a downright standstill. Jacob's grandmother, who he had been extremely close to, passed away. Melissa didn't actually mention Jacob losing his grandmother when she came into session expressing alarm over a sudden shift in Jacob's behavior. He wasn't doing anything really wrong per se, but something about his energy seemed different to her in a way that she couldn't quite put her finger on. Jacob insisted whenever she would ask that everything was fine. It wasn't until Jacob told her that he wouldn't be accompanying her to her friend's wedding that Melissa finally reached her breaking point. They'd had a terrible fight where Melissa pointed out that she couldn't be in a relationship with a man who didn't show up for her.

"I told him that I needed him to suck it up and come to this wedding with me! I mean, it's bad enough being the last of my friends to get engaged, but now I'm supposed to sit there all by myself, swearing to everyone that I have a boyfriend. He can't even make me a priority for one weekend of his life? I mean Jesus, I know he's sad that his grandmother died, but come on!" I remember feeling surprised when Melissa brought up his grandmother. This was the first I was hearing of her. "What do you know about his grandmother?" I probed.

"I mean. I get it. He was really close to her. His mom was an alcoholic and he went to live with his grandmother when he was six. He basically grew up without knowing who his dad was, so his grandmother ended up being like a mom and dad to him. She still lived in Michigan up until she died. And I know he'd been trying to get back there to spend time with her, but his job is kind of intense. So I mean, I understand why he feels bad. And I offered to go with him to the funeral, but he's just completely shutting me out," Melissa explained.

As I painted the picture in my head of the emotions he must be experiencing, I began to feel an immense amount of sadness. Melissa must've sensed this by the look on my face, because she seemed to slowly start putting puzzle pieces together in her head. "Oh God," she said. "I've been so caught up in this 'last single woman' BS, that I didn't even think about how much pain he must be in. He kept insisting that he was fine and I guess I just wanted to believe that it was true. So I left him alone."

The attempts Melissa made to repair things between them ended up being futile. Jacob was grateful to her for her remorse and for her expressing that she'd let him down by not understanding the severity of his grief. But ultimately, he felt that there had been a depth of connection missing between them that he didn't feel interested in trying to force. Melissa was absolutely devastated—mostly because she felt a colossal sense of shame for treating one of the kindest men she'd ever dated the way she treated Jacob. But Melissa wasn't a callous person, nor was she intentionally disregarding what Jacob was going through. She was caught up in the panic that often ensues for women as they age in a society that teaches them that their worth lies in their ability to be chosen, and that their market value literally decreases a little bit more every year.

When Melissa met Jacob, she wasn't present. She wasn't feeling grounded in her sense of self, and therefore wasn't ready to consciously invite another person into her life. She wasn't focused on getting to know Jacob for the truth of who he was. She didn't see him as a unique Soul on his own path to experience what he was meant to learn and experience in this lifetime. She was focused on finding someone who could fill the role of *her* boyfriend, who would shortly become *her* fiancé, and would then take on the role of *her* husband. Very shortly after their initial meeting, she came into session and proclaimed that she had met *her* husband. But how could she know that? How could she know whether or not someone would be the right fit as a life partner so soon after meeting them? Of course, she couldn't know. She projected onto Jacob her need to fill the space in her life that she felt desperate to fill. Like so many of us, Melissa was taught that the most important thing for a woman to do is to seal the deal. To lock things down. To "make them *mine*."

But this is not unique to the experience of women. Regardless of our gender, our sexual orientation, or the structure of our relationships, we've been taught to understand that some sort of declaration that we "belong to one another" is what solidifies a romantic partnership as being real. And let me clear: this is not a stance against monogamous relationships. Quite the contrary. I think that the safety and containment of a grounded partnership can offer us the roots from which we are able to truly take flight in our lives. But I do believe that there's a human tendency to take love for granted once we believe that we've reached a point of arrival with another person.

It almost starts to feel like a game. We achieve certain levels—or stages of relationship—and once we've reached the culmination of the game, the understanding is that we will be gifted with another human being. It feels a bit strange to be playing games with something so sacred. The act of loving is the closest thing to experiencing Divinity each of us can do while we're alive. Dating apps, the commercialization of weddings, and a framework of love that focuses on the responsibility of another to "meet our needs" in a satisfactory way has taught us to see those we attempt to love as a means to an end. It's taught us to buy into a distorted vision of love that encourages us to further disconnect from our Souls.

Not About Me, and Yet, All About Me

I often tell my clients that it's an incredibly empowering thing to realize that there's actually no feeling we can feel that will kill us. This is meant to serve as a reminder that our feelings are meant to be felt, and that it's normally the resistance to feeling the feelings that are coming to the surface that compounds our experience of suffering. I can stand by this statement while simultaneously holding the awareness that anyone who's ever felt the intestine-churning, gut-wrenching, unable-to-find-your-next-breath experience of a heartbreak has known feelings that seem as though they could actually be the cause of your demise. This feeling of heartbreak can come from a variety of losses: the death of a loved one, the forfeiture of innocence after a betrayal, the ostracization from a community, or the heartbreak that seems to overshadow all the others—the love we feel for someone who cannot (for whatever reason) reciprocate that love.

When we believe that we love someone whom we perceive as having a great deal of worth (we respect their way of moving through the world, we feel an immense physical attraction, and we see a clear vision of how our lives would be enhanced by being in partnership with this person), our ego mind forms an attachment to the idea that this person holds something that we believe we lack. They are responsible for the positive feelings we feel in their presence. Winning their love would offer us a sense of accomplishment, fulfillment, and belonging. These are all examples of the ways that we objectify another person, making them the means to an end point of our personal fulfillment. The ego decides that they're "the one" because the ego advocates for scarcity and fear. It believes that there's a scarcity of people we could conceivably meet and have a sacred connection with. It exacerbates the fear that we will never feel the feelings this person aroused within us again.

But here's the difficult truth. None of this is really about the person we believe we're in love with. This is demonstrated when the object of our affection does not return the feelings we'd like for them to feel. There's a particular flavor about what it brings up within us, to feel that we are not being chosen. If what we were feeling were *truly* about this other person, we would desire to see and understand them clearly. We would respect the truth of their feelings, even if they were contradictory to our own. We would trust in the timing of two hearts colliding with a mutual desire to build a relationship. But our ego defends against this level of clarity because it wants to take possession of the object it believes will make it feel good.

We live in a culture that's taught us that when something has great value, it's our job to hustle for it—we have to earn it. We believe that if someone we see as holding a great deal of worth rejects us, it's our job to try harder. We have to work to prove to them that we are worthy of their love. This desire to prove we are worthy of the love we desire is rooted in an attachment wound, and ultimately an indication of our detachment from our inner feminine.

When our love for another is rooted in masculine principles, we seek to calm our experience of inner turbulence by focusing our thoughts on the object of our desire. We attempt to **contain** the rapturous magnetism of eros in a way that feels accessible to us—whenever we desire it. But the very nature of eros is rooted in aliveness, and to that end, the moment we attempt to box in something that is meant to be expansive, it will feel stifled, unresponsive, and lifeless.

If our love for another is rooted in principles of the feminine, however, love is collaborative and sourced from a foundation of trust. The trust that we feel is less about the actions of the other person, but in the Divine timing of life's rhythms and unfolding. We understand that *true love* for another person means never attempting to clutch, control, or constrain them in a place that they don't have a desire to be. It's love that continues to honor the free will of the other, long after two people have partnered.

But the embodiment of this as a practice can be unbelievably confronting. It requires a reckoning with the ego mind in a way that can feel like a death. And to an extent, it feels that way because it is. We are shedding a limited, fear-based, externally focused construct of love in exchange for an expansive, trusting, seasoned understanding of how to be in relationship with another. A love that consistently brings the focus back to the only person we get to have any control over in this life—ourselves. It's a love rooted in taking personal responsibility for using our relationships as a mirror. This mirror shows us where there is space for growth and accountability through the moments when we feel a sense of activation. This is where love has the potential to alchemize our suffering into our emancipation, by seeing every scenario that love brings to the surface as a beacon, guiding us back home to our (capital S) Selves. Once we've done enough self-exploration to realize that all points of activation are meant to lead us back to the path of personal responsibility, we're able to utilize the tools we've acquired to start integrating the elements of our internal masculine and feminine.

Stage Three

SOVEREIGN

CHAPTER 8

Reclaiming the Masculine

"learning to wear a mask (that word already embedded
in the term 'masculinity') is the first lesson in patriarchal
masculinity that a boy learns. asked to give up the true self in
order to realize the patriarchal ideal, boys learn self-betrayal
early and are rewarded for these acts of soul murder."

BELL HOOKS

Boys Are Taught Not to Feel, Girls Are Taught Not to Care

here's a truth that feels painfully difficult to admit. Before I became the
mother to a son, I didn't have a great deal of curiosity about the inner
landscape of men. Maybe I thought about how easy I believed it was
to manipulate them into behaving in the ways that I wanted them to
behave. I thought about what I perceived to be a lack of emotional savvy
and curiosity within them. I thought about the shortsighted decisions
they seemed to make and how those decisions caused women pain. But I
never gave much thought to what it must feel like to inhabit the skin of
a man in a patriarchal society.

I was certainly aware of the differences in how my brother and I were
raised in the same household; him being raised to be tough and responsible in a world that wouldn't give a damn about his sensitivity or hurts,
me being raised to hold the dichotomies of the strength I would need to
embody as a Black woman—beside the limitations a patriarchal culture
engrains in all women (prioritizing being chosen, questioning my own
innate wisdom, and making myself and my needs small).

But like most women, I spent so much of my life focused on the injustices this society imposed upon my personhood that I never gave much thought to the damage that a domination-based system inflicts on men. I never thought about what happens inside the Soul of a little boy the first time he's made fun of on the school playground because he "throws like a girl," or is wearing something that the other boys deem effeminate. I never considered how that same little boy might internalize the contempt he senses in the gaze of his father when that father witnesses him experiencing the emotions he was trained to detach from long ago.

We live in a society that teaches men that masculinity is something that is meant to be performed, and that this performance resembles a sort of stoicism and suppression of a great deal of who you are. There is a role that little boys are taught that they are meant to play. They are not meant to be "all in their feelings." They are meant to see women as conquests and trophies to acquire. They are meant to seek power and external recognition. They are meant to enjoy "guy things" like aggression, sports bars, and being in constant competition with others. But more than anything else, they are not meant to be vulnerable—and what is considered vulnerable is often the equivalent of allowing themselves to be hurt, fully seen, afraid, unsure, or anything that might be perceived by others as weak.

Most women have not been socialized to hold much empathy for the emotional challenges modern men are confronted with. Modern feminism has taught us that elevating women out of patriarchal oppression depends upon our ability to hold men accountable for their behavior. And to a certain extent, that's very true. But also, men and a system of patriarchy are not synonymous with one another. Many of the men we're seeking to hold accountable (for the objectification of women, a fundamental lack of equality, violence and misogyny that have caused immeasurable pain, and an inability to hold all aspects of the feminine with a sense of dignity and respect) have also been raised in and deeply harmed by the same patriarchal structures.

What's worse is that they're harmed by this system without being consciously aware of the ways they're being damaged. In her book *The Will to Change: Men, Masculinity, and Love*, bell hooks points out that,

"Feminist advocates collude in the pain of men wounded by patriarchy when they falsely represent men as always and only powerful, as always and only gaining privileges from their blind obedience to patriarchy. But as long as men are brainwashed to equate violent domination and abuse of women with privilege, they will have no understanding of the damage done to themselves or to others, and no motivation to change."[1]

A patriarchal structure teaches men that their innate worth lies in their ability to be respected by others as men. Men are taught that they can earn external respect (which essentially boils down to the love and acceptance that all human animals long to feel) in one of three ways:

- **Through the celebration of aggression and violence or defense of their honor**

  This doesn't necessarily mean being physically violent themselves; it can be in the celebration of their connection and knowledge of more "manly" sports like football over sports which also require a great deal of physical prowess (like gymnastics or golf) but are considered by society to be less masculine.

- **Through the accumulation of material wealth or power**

  Respect can be sought through the constant striving for material assets—a man who amasses a great deal of wealth or notoriety is considered better equipped to provide for a family, to leverage his power as a means to protect others, and is sometimes even described by society as a "high-value man."

- **Through sexual prowess and the ability to dominate and objectify women**

  Images of successful men with a "trophy wife" on their arm, or celebrating on a yacht with a plethora of submissive young women adorning the environment like ornaments, reinforce the idea that societal respect is earned by treating women not as equal in their humanity, but as objects that demonstrate to others your level of success.

It feels easy to say that a "good man" would disregard such surface-level templates of what it means to be a man. But in order to challenge these aspects of our societal programming, it becomes incumbent on all of us (yes, women too) to be vigorously honest with ourselves. We have to look at the ways that we've perpetuated gender norms in our own lives when we've benefited from them. We have to tell the truth about ways we've shamed men for their vulnerability and inability to adhere to gender stereotypes. And we have to have a hard look at where we've dismissed their experience of internalized shame when they were deemed less than "manly," and how that has shaped the safety they've felt living in their own skin (or lack thereof).

Shortly after my marriage ended, I was sitting in therapy outlining for my therapist all of the reasons that I felt confident that I was actually better off without a man in my life. "Maybe I'm just not the type of person who wants to spend my life compromising who I am, and what I want to do with my time. Maybe some people are better off living without constantly considering a partner. Maybe I'm not willing to diminish the truth of who I am ever again. Maybe this is just better!" After I finished nearly shouting my case in favor of hyper-independence at her, I looked up to see my therapist looking at me with a sadness in her eyes that surprised and frankly irritated me. What was she so sad about? I was awake, empowered, and clear that the attempt to be in relationships with men had been a losing strategy all along. What was her problem?

"Dené, let me ask you something," she said calmly. "How many men in your life would you say that you really felt like you could trust?" Her words felt like a sucker punch in my gut. All of a sudden, I began crying what felt like a lifetime's worth of tears. And the funny thing is, to a certain extent they were the tears of several lifetimes. It's like I was crying on behalf of an entire lineage of women before me. I was crying tears of grief over the distorted relationship that I (like so many women, and my own ancestors before me) had with the masculine. This pain is generational. Every part of my training up to this point had taught me to be guarded, self-contained, and forever suspicious of men—even the men in my life who went above and beyond to prove themselves to be trustworthy. I was taught, like so many other women, to wear a wounded masculine armor, and to see feminine qualities like openness and trust as liabilities. This is the generational pain we've been carrying as women. Women have been so deeply harmed in various ways by wounded masculine energy that we've learned to carry a low-level defensiveness into our relationships, often beyond the reality of what we may be experiencing.

I will be the first to take ownership of the fact that for much of my own life, I would've heard someone speak about the same men's issues I'm speaking of without much interest in why they should be my concern. I was so consumed with the self-righteousness of a woman who'd been disregarded by a patriarchal society. Even in my early work as a therapist, I held a sense of curiosity about men's behavior with a psychological distance, and consistently dismissed the complexity of a man's inner landscape in my personal relationships.

And then . . . I had a little boy. This little being changed everything. He was the closest thing to perfection, purity, and goodness that I'd ever known. My connection to his tender vulnerability was undeniable from the moment I knew he was on his way. Suddenly I felt desperate to consider how his little heart would be impacted by every single decision I made. I would be his first experience of nurturance and connection, and that meant taking radical responsibility for his earliest experience of a core feminine energy—me.

My little boy became the catalyst for an inner reckoning. I had to have an honest look at how I'd been in relationship to masculine energy as a whole up to this point. I couldn't expect him to have reciprocal, safe, loving relationships with women (in whatever form that might take) if that's not what he grew up having modeled for him. How could I raise a trustworthy man if I had a fundamental lack of trust in men? How could I teach him that each and every one of us are worthy of being treated with dignity and respect if that wasn't the deepest truth of how I was interacting with one half of our society?

The emotions that came to the surface in my therapist's office served as a clear indication that I was hungry to put down my masculine shield. Some part of me wanted to soften into a different kind of relationship with masculine energy. I wanted to believe that it was possible for me to experience safe, authentic, reciprocal love with a man. But the truth of the matter was, I had no idea how to do that. I knew that if I wanted to teach my little boy about the tremendous gift his presence was to this world, I would have to hold all men with the same level of reverence that I would want for him. I can see now that the Universe gifted me with being the mama to this precious baby boy as an invitation to heal my relationship with men. There was so much about men that I didn't understand, but that I suddenly felt desperate to see.

Anger, Isolation, and Sex

Human animals are emotional beings. But our society offers men a very limited range of emotional expressions that are considered permissible. This can feel a bit confusing, because in many ways, current cultural narratives suggest that we've moved beyond archaic concepts of alpha males and stoicism in favor of men who are celebrated for their sensitivity and emotional intelligence. And while we may celebrate men who exhibit a certain level of thoughtfulness, a certain range of presence, and a capacity for emotional exploration, the larger truth is that we are still a society that sends men some very strong messaging about the dangers of being "overly" emotional, vulnerable, and especially about exhibiting mental health struggles. I can think of several very recent examples (as I write this in the year 2023) of an outpouring of social media memes poking fun at male celebrities who were clearly exhibiting signs that they were struggling with their mental health.

We prefer that men be sensitive—but not scared. Overt in their compassion for others—but not overwhelmed by the pressure to succeed and provide. Willing to be open about the truth of how they're feeling—but certainly not needy and making their problems someone else's problems to solve. So many of the impossible standards society places upon men are almost identical to the set of wounded masculine expectations placed upon women. So when men fail to measure up to these standards, they are met with an enormous level of contempt—normally from women just as much as other men. Because we are only capable of holding the humanity of others with the same level of compassion that we are able to hold for our own.

The truth of the matter is we don't have a lot of clear representations of healthy masculinity in our modern world. Mostly because the modern world is still operating within an extremely wounded masculine paradigm. Without clear examples of what it looks like to feel, identify, safely process, and release the multitude of emotions a man will inevitably feel, men are forced to metabolize their emotional terrain in one of the few ways society has deemed acceptable: suppression, aggression, or sex.

The **suppression** of a man's emotions can look like minimizing, compartmentalizing, numbing, isolating, or distracting. Society has taught men that seeking support for their emotional struggles equates to weakness. At most, they may attempt to share some of what they are feeling with their partner, but the same programming that has infiltrated men has often influenced those they are in partnerships with. Some of the most damaging feedback a man can receive is in the shaming that occurs when he attempts to be vulnerable with someone who doesn't have the emotional tools or capacity to hold space for his vulnerability.

Aggression—within reason—is definitely viewed as a societally acceptable form of processing for men. Fathers encourage their sons "not to be a punk" when someone is bullying them on the playground. Men pick fights in bars with those who are rooting for an opposing sports team. Many attribute this propensity for aggression to fact that men have more testosterone. But that fails to acknowledge the public humiliation a little boy experiences when he is encouraged to fight when he doesn't want to. He is deemed soft, weak, or "less than a man" if and when he commits the ultimate sin in the eyes of patriarchal manhood and begins to cry. Very specific moments of humiliation often created the foundation of a male tendency to detach from the fullness of their own humanity.

And then there's **sex**. There's a fundamental distortion in the way that society has co-opted a man's relationship to his own sensuality. This is, at its core, his relationship to his own feminine essence. And while we have been conditioned to believe that men are extremely sexual beings and as such would inevitably be in touch with their own sensuality, when we teach men that their self-worth is connected to their ability to have as much sex as possible (and I might add, without exhibiting signs of being emotionally attached to the person they're having sex with), we teach them to use the pleasure centers that fire during sex as a way to self-regulate. Sex becomes one of the few socially acceptable spaces where men get to experience tenderness, present centered aliveness, and access any kind of emotional release. The experience of this outlet can become extremely addictive in a society that offers men very few containers for emotional vulnerability. Their relationship with sex (either with others or quite often through the use of pornography) becomes similar to the relationship an addict has with their drug of choice—an unconscious compulsion forms to serve as a distraction from difficult emotions they feel ill-equipped to feel.

I met Alfie and Julia in the midst of a marital crisis. They were in their late thirties, had been married for four years, and Julia was finally pregnant—twelve weeks, to be exact—after their third round of IVF and having struggled to conceive since shortly after they were married. Julia had always wanted to be a mother, and was certain that finding the man she wanted to be with was going to be the most challenging aspect of achieving her lifelong goal. Their struggle to conceive had been taxing on their relationship, to say the least, and they came to see me shortly after Julia discovered that Alfie had been involved in several extramarital affairs throughout their relationship.

The first couple of sessions with Julia and Alfie felt like triage. We couldn't even begin to understand what had happened or what to do next until we established a foundation for how each of them could continue breathing as they were confronted with the worst-case scenario that they could possibly imagine. And I say *each of them* in this situation quite deliberately. Julia had certainly been unceremoniously catapulted into the unspeakable reality of carrying a baby for a man she didn't even recognize, but Alfie was also confronted with the inability to hide from aspects of himself any longer. He was forced to face an internal split he had used as a survival mechanism for years—the version of himself he allowed the world to see (the nice guy, the marrying type, the one who had always provided stability and safety for everyone in his life) and the shadow aspect of who he was (the man with an inability to control himself when confronted by various forms of lust and temptation, and whose hatred for himself grew bigger with each sexual encounter, disgusted that he was completely powerless to make himself stop).

I decided to frame my work with Julia and Alfie in the same way I would a couple grappling with any other addiction, because from my perspective, Alfie's addiction to impulsive behaviors was the larger issue here than the infidelity. I suggested that both of them connect with a twelve-step community—Alfie, a sex and love addiction community, and Julia, a codependency support community. This suggestion may feel like an uncharacteristic response to a couple facing serial infidelity, but here's what I've come to understand about relationships. Relationships are *always* a two-way street. Quite often when there's infidelity in a relationship, the couples therapy centers on making the person who stepped out of the relationship the IP (identified patient) and creates a strategy for how they can rebuild a sense of trust. But this is just like putting a Band-Aid on a gaping, unaddressed wound. It misses an opportunity for both people to address the deeper layers of dysfunction in their relationship dynamic that manifested as an affair.

There is simply no way that Julia could be in a relationship with a man who had been carrying around this level of secrecy throughout the entire duration of their relationship without a normalized lack of emotional intimacy between them. This is not about removing the responsibility Alfie held for committing this level of betrayal so much as it's about attempting to understand the larger ecosystem of their relationship. What were the unspoken contracts they were each playing out in their dynamic—and possibly even rebelling against?

Taking this approach to the work brought up a great deal of understandable resistance from Julia. This was when I laid out for her what I saw as her two options. Option one—she could leave this man. She could do her own grief work, focus her energy on being the best mom possible, and hopefully reach a point where she could amicably co-parent with the father of her child. Option two—she could work to understand how this happened, but *really* attempt to understand. I would not collude with her in painting herself as the helpless victim of a monster who had deliberately impregnated her and trapped her into a marriage to destroy her life. She had options—she could stay or she could go. It would be hard either way, but this was one of those moments where she would have to take responsibility for her choice.

Julia decided that she wanted to work to understand. Not only to understand her dynamic with Alfie, but everything she had been taught about men, women, and relationships—and what she began to see as a pattern of losing herself as an individual every time she entered a relationship with another person. She started asking herself some really difficult questions. Questions like: where had she consistently made her needs small and held herself back from speaking about what rubbed her the wrong way in an attempt to maintain her connection to another person? Where had she been so preoccupied with biological clocks and comparing herself to others that she'd lost track of being present in what she truly wanted for herself? How might this unbelievably painful realization about Alfie serve as a rock-bottom moment, offering the two of them a solid foundation on which to build from—one based on radical transparency and truth?

Julia eventually realized that there had been an unspoken agreement between she and Alfie from the moment they met. She wouldn't force him to talk about the lack of emotional intimacy that had (in retrospect) always been there between them. And in return, he would play the role of the perfect, submissive husband, willing to go along with whatever she desired. Acknowledging her part in this agreement actually felt empowering for Julia. It became a way for her to acknowledge for herself that she was nobody's victim. She might have made herself and her needs small in the past because that was what she had been taught to do. But now that she could see it, she couldn't unsee it. She might have been willing to trade emotional safety for the security of having a partner by her side in the past, but now that she could see it for what it was, she was unwilling to do that ever again.

Julia's commitment to the process seemed to initiate a sense of determination in Alfie. He started attending a twelve-step meeting every morning in addition to doing his own individual weekly therapy. What was most profound to witness Alfie speak about was the transformational experience of being held by the brotherhood of men he found in his twelve-step work. These men shared about their own pain, fears, and experiences of loneliness in a way that reflected back to Alfie feelings he had thought he was alone in feeling his entire life. They helped him understand that he'd used sex as a distraction since he was a teenager to cope with unprocessed pain. The experience of getting attention from girls became a euphoric one—almost like the feeling he'd felt when he used drugs.

He realized that he never really cultivated a relationship with himself outside of how he was experienced by other people. If he was popular with the girls in his class, he believed he was good. If he was dating a popular girl (one that the rest of his peers envied him for being with), not only was he able to cultivate a brief distraction from his compulsive desire for sex with multiple girls for a while, but he found a sense of identity in being her boyfriend. These codependent ways of relating to others are a large part of why I often say that codependency is the most pervasive (and rarely acknowledged) form of addiction in our society.

What's also important to understand about healthy polarity with a woman for a core masculine man like Alfie is that operating in this level of codependency (outsourcing of identity, getting a hit of feel-good chemicals from being seen or desired, using relationships as a distraction from feeling uncomfortable or cultivating a clear life mission) is wounded feminine energy. This became a substantial roadblock in the cultivation of healthy polarity between Alfie and Julia, and explained why some of the dynamics between them were unsustainable.

Alfie started to unpack all of this in our sessions as well as with the brotherhood of men he met with regularly. What eventually came to the surface was an incredible amount of anger. He started to see the amount of the pressure he'd felt to step up as the man of the house when his father had unceremoniously left his mother high and dry. As much as he loved his mother, taking on the role of the surrogate man in her life had left him with an unprocessed rage toward women that he'd spent a lifetime pushing down.

He shared with Julia and I that during a camping trip with a group of men, they'd asked him to share about everything that made him angry. Once Alfie got started, he didn't think he'd ever stop. He was furious with his father for being a coward, leaving him with no guidebook on how to be a self-respecting man. He felt incensed by his mother's constant need for him—confused by why his role as her "golden boy" always felt like more of a burden then a gift. He felt angry with every woman he'd ever been in a relationship with, including Julia, for treating him like a lap dog—there to be of service to them without caring about what he thought or how he truly felt.

The more time he spent talking about his anger with other men, he found that what he was most angry about was how much effort he'd put into abandoning himself. And that while he'd experienced a sort of tension release while having sex with the different women he'd been with, most of the time what he wanted from them was just someone to talk to who wouldn't judge him for being weak, overwhelmed, or afraid. He realized that underneath his anger was a lifetime of unprocessed grief that the little boy inside of him had learned to stuff down in service of his ability to "be a man." In his marriage to Julia, Alfie had attempted to marry the "good girl" in the hopes that it would cap his insatiable lust for other women and give him a sense of identity in being the "good husband" that those around him could admire. This plan backfired when Alfie's complete submission to Julia's leadership put her in the position of mothering her husband (wounded masculine energy) and killing off any sort of authentic erotic charge between them.

Being surrounded by a brotherhood of men allowed Alfie to feel that every part of his humanity was welcome in their presence, while also holding him accountable for stepping into his healthy masculine core—cultivating a sense of discipline and learning to stay with himself through waves of uncomfortable emotions, challenging himself to step out of his comfort zone physically and emotionally to demonstrate to himself what he was capable of, and identifying a clear mission for his life. Alfie realized he needed clarity about who *he wanted* to be, and to start showing up as the man he knew in his Soul he was capable of being.

All of the work both Alfie and Julia were doing brought a whole new dynamic into their relationship. Each of them cultivated a sense of Self that they hadn't brought into the union when they first got married. Over time, Alfie began to take on a leadership role in the men's groups he attended; he found that supporting other men with what he'd come to understand about himself filled him with a sense of meaning that left him wanting to do more. Eventually Alfie went back to graduate school to become a therapist who specialized in men's work. He and Julia welcomed a beautiful baby boy, and I watched as the two of them transformed their relationship into one filled with a deep sense of trust and respect for one another. They went from two shell-shocked strangers armored up and terrified to be seen by the other to a couple that I've held as one of the most beautiful demonstrations of what can be created when we commit to unearthing our pain.

From my perspective, Alfie and Julia's dilemma represents the most common issue that comes to the surface when two people attempt to join together in partnership without having any idea of who they truly are as individuals. When two people come into relationship without a sense of (capital S) Self—meaning what they want to do with their life and why, what the bottom-line ethics they stand behind are, and the ways they've walked through their own personal fires, proving to themselves what they are capable of—they seek to outsource their sense of identity in their relationship. Our sense of identity cannot live within the container of our relationship to another person. Each of us are responsible for knowing and defining who we choose to be in this life for ourselves.

Society offers us some convoluted ways of processing a man's actions when he does something like what Alfie did early in his relationship with Julia. They say, "Boys will be boys," or, "Men just can't control themselves," or attribute this kind of behavior to him being a fundamentally bad person. This sends us the collective message that masculine energy is unfocused, undisciplined, and fundamentally unsafe. If Alfie and Julia had stayed together without Alfie cultivating a solid understanding of why he was using sex as a subterfuge for difficult emotions, the behavior pattern would have more than likely continued, with each of them perpetuating the wounds that drew them to one another to begin with.

I don't believe in people being fundamentally bad or irredeemable. I'd certainly be in the wrong line of work if I did. But beyond that, I believe that just as we are wounded by relationships, we have the propensity to be healed in relationships. A society that calls men toxic without attempting to understand the wounded little boys that those toxic behaviors are often acting in defense of, has no hope of supporting men like Alfie in becoming who they have the potential to be. We see behaviors like aggression or hypersexuality in a man and think those traits define who this person is, when in reality, they are like warning signals desperately pointing to the repression of unprocessed pain within them.

Harvesting Feminine Energy

There's a challenging element of relational dynamics that shows up specifically in heterosexual relationships and can be kind of difficult to talk about. I've found that it's specific to heterosexual gender norms because of how men and women are socialized. This dynamic becomes one of the long-term implications of a society that teaches women that they are a commodifiable object and that their worth lies in their ability to be chosen by a man. This conditions women to unconsciously withhold vital aspects of who they are out of fear that the full range of their humanity will make them less desirable. It also conditions men to believe that they are meant to be the center of a woman's universe in a way that isn't necessarily based on her deepest truth.

When a woman meets and desires to be in relationship with a man, she will quite often focus all of her energetic attention on him. She will make his needs her priority, delicately consider his feelings in the truths she chooses to share, focus her attention on what he finds appealing, and do whatever else is required to be the type of woman a man would want to "settle down" with. Historically, it's been society that has taught her to do this. She's been conditioned to believe that if she reaches her mid-thirties without being singled out as worthy enough to be chosen, there is something wrong with her. Meanwhile, her male counterparts of the same age are revered and coveted as the unattainable bachelor. Some of these gender dynamics are shifting as women are owning their worth and pushing back on patriarchal narratives. But this programming runs deep, and society still makes the assumption that a single man past a certain age has made a choice, while a single woman past a certain age has not been chosen.

This social conundrum often impacts the level of transparency women bring into the early stages of a relationship with a man. She isn't necessarily making a conscious decision to withhold, but in many ways, she's acting in alignment with what she believes to be true at the time. But the truths we feel when we are attempting to secure an attachment (especially with what we've been taught romantic attachments should look and feel like) have a tendency to shift once that relationship feels solidified.

I often hear married men express feeling like they were "duped" by the shift they experience with a woman once they have committed to her. Before they make the decision to get married, they remember being treated like a king. This woman was captivated by everything they had to say. She regularly wore sexy lingerie and was incredibly receptive to their sexual advances. What made him want to marry her was the fact that she was his ride or die—believing in her man, his dreams, and taking on the role of his biggest cheerleader. And then after a few years of marriage—especially in relationships where children have come into the picture—all of that abruptly comes to a halt.

Here are the deeper layers of what I believe is happening between these men and women. So much of what a man is experiencing from this woman in those early interactions is her healthy feminine energy. Her nurturing essence, her grand vision of what he is capable of, her ability to inspire sensuality and affection, her ability to trust and receive from him, how she connects at the level of her heart, her willingness to surrender to him, her radiance and beauty, and her longing for more of all that he is. These elements of the feminine are aroused when she feels seen, held, and appreciated by the masculine. Society has taught men that these feminine energetics exist for the purpose of a man's pleasure. That they are bottomless energetics to be harvested by men without these same men holding any responsibility for what is required to continue to cultivate this energy.

Men draw feminine energy from the women in their lives in a way that makes *them* feel worthy, validated, and loved. But in a perfect world, men would not be taught to use women as the main resource for this type of feminine nurturance. Ideally the foundation for this type of nurturance and validation in a man's life would come from his caretakers. A man's foundational experiences would encourage him to explore and respect the full range of his emotions. He would be allowed to value *his* radiance, *his* lightheartedness, *his* sensuality and *his* right to play. He would be taught to believe in his innate value—simply because of who he is. But this is not the society we live in. In a society that teaches him that he is meant to draw these elements solely from an external source, he learns that women are meant to be his abundant resource for drawing this type of energy.

This is an unspoken agreement that occurs in exchange for a patriarchal society's requirement that men sever themselves from their emotions. They don't have to hold and process the complexity of what they're feeling—the women in their lives will do it for them. This might show up as a mother who instills patriarchal values and encourages a lack of personal responsibility in her son. Or in a man's continuous attempt to compensate for a lack of childhood nurturance in all of his relationships with women. Either way, society teaches women that they are meant to pick up where a maternal figure in a man's life left off, or offer the nurturing acknowledgment that he's been seeking for a lifetime.

But this creates a significant issue in relationships. Society's insistence that women hold the capacity to nurture men in a maternal way misunderstands one very important aspect of motherhood. It often takes women, for a period of time, out of their feminine. For women, the embodied experience of mothering is an extremely masculine energetic. It's the work of creating safety, structure, protection, and assurance. When a man looks to a core feminine woman to provide him with a sense of emotional assurance, she can take on this maternal role with him to a point, but a core feminine woman will instinctively start to resent embodying the more masculine role in their dynamic over time.

This dynamic can be very hard for women to be honest about, mostly because it is so deeply engrained in a woman's conditioning to protect men from the ways we view them unfavorably. As we talked about previously, this is for a very specific reason. Women defend the egos of men in an attempt to keep themselves safe. Clearly stating what she views as a lack of competence, strength, or prowess within him can be (and in many cases has been) a dangerous situation for a woman to place herself in. If not a physically dangerous situation, certainly one that could put her relational attachment in jeopardy.

This is one of those gender dynamics that's really nobody's fault, but it certainly creates a problem. Both men and women are simply acting out what they didn't get in childhood in their partnerships, without understanding how playing these roles impacts how they feel about each other over time. I can clearly recall this dynamic in my own marriage, but at the time, I didn't have the language or the insight to even understand what was happening between us. And what makes it even more difficult to understand or identify is that these energetic dynamics are not constant. There were many moments when my husband did occupy a masculine, containing space in our dynamic. But when it came to the understanding of his own emotional landscape, I could feel him often expecting me to provide a sense of maternal containment.

Many couples don't have a clear recognition of the complexity of this issue until after they have their first baby. The physical and psychological shift that occurs within a woman literally puts her into survival mode. She suddenly has zero tolerance for another adult pulling on her energetic resources. She already feels completely depleted and disconnected from her ability to connect to her feminine. She is looking for him to attune to her and support in the replenishment of this energy. She is longing to be reminded of the feminine essence she can't feel when she is inundated by the masculine tasks of motherhood. But as long as a man depends solely on his woman for his emotional reassurance, she will begin to view him as another child.

Abbie understood this dynamic far too well. After a twenty-year marriage to a man who was emotionally abusive, who she supported financially, and who suggested that she was responsible for every wrong turn his life had ever taken, she reached a breaking point and realized that not only did she want to be free from this marriage, but from the childhood wounds that had caused her to stay in a relationship like this for so long.

I met Abbie at a retreat I was facilitating shortly after she left her husband—shell-shocked, terrified, and without any sense of what life would look like on her own. A year later, I ran into her again, and to say she had undergone a cataclysmic transformation by the time we met the second time would be a vast understatement. I didn't even recognize her. She was positively radiant. She did a deep dive into several different healing modalities—talk therapy, EMDR, yoga, meditation, neurogenic tremoring, therapeutic bodywork, and so much more. She was fully committed to the process of reclaiming her life and was falling in love with remembering who she was. She became clear about how good life could be when she remembered how powerful she was on her own.

Abbie had also been empowered by rediscovering herself as a sexual being. After almost twenty years of believing that sex was something she didn't care much about, she was delighted to discover that not only did she care about sex, but that the sex she was having in her newfound sense of liberation was like nothing that she'd experienced before. She felt lighter, free, intuitive, sensual, curious, hopeful, and able to trust herself again. Essentially, she had reclaimed her feminine essence.

Abbie spent over a year casually dating and focusing her energy on her own healing and integrative work—and then she met Drew. Abbie felt an immediate sense of safety with Drew. He too was divorced, and was warm and transparent. He shared her love of being outdoors and was present and thoughtful in the way that he pursued her. I remember her once noting that he was nothing like her ex-husband and that she was finding so much healing in the realization that men could be tender, clear, and willing to focus on her needs. And whoa—was the sex with him incredible. In the beginning, Drew felt like the manifestation of everything Abbie could possibly want in a relationship. He was there for her when she needed support, he was open to her suggestions and point of view, and he expressed his devotion and desire for them to take their relationship to the next level.

But after several months of dating, Abbie started to feel something shift in the way she felt around Drew. She couldn't understand why something about their dynamic was suddenly making her feel suffocated. One night, they got in a fight about Abbie's unwillingness to talk about the future, and Abbie described herself having a visceral reaction of contempt coming out of her towards Drew. He had simply expressed that he didn't know if he could tolerate the ambiguity of them not putting a plan in place for where the relationship was going. Almost immediately after she left him, Abbie called one of the other men she'd been sleeping with before they met, and slept with him that same night. Something about the conversation she had with Drew made her feel like a caged animal, in the same way she'd felt throughout the majority of her marriage. I was instantly captivated as she told me the story.

It was true that Drew was kind and openhearted with Abbie in a way her husband hadn't been, but there was something familiar about their dynamic that she couldn't quite put her finger on. I asked Abbie to give me some examples of things he did that made her feel like something was off. She described the way he was always checking in about the decisions he made. Whether it was what he was going to have for lunch, how to handle a conversation with a colleague, or which shirt would be more appropriate for an afternoon BBQ they were attending—it was almost as if Drew felt he needed Abbie's cosign before he could move forward with any of the decisions he made. She also noticed that when she wasn't available to offer him her two cents, he would survey the other women in his life. Always the women. His female friends, his sister, sometimes even his ex-wife.

But in addition to this tendency to seek direction from others, Drew didn't have a whole lot going on in his own life. He had been forced to retire early from his previous career, and had made enough money in the settlement that he didn't need to work. And while Abbie was often making suggestions about what Drew could do with his time, he always seemed to rebuff her suggestions with a reason why what she was saying wasn't possible. Abbie had her own career, and her own money. She had kids of her own to take care of, and was perfectly capable of doing it. She wasn't looking for Drew to take care of her financially, but something about his lack of direction caused her to view him as childlike and unsure of himself. These were energetics that felt reminiscent of the dynamic with her ex-husband. He'd always had a reason why something wasn't possible, and why she didn't understand how hard it was for him to move forward with the execution of a plan.

The more Abbie and I talked about it, the more I could see what was playing out in her relationship with Drew. This convolution of healthy polarity and the fact that Drew was using Abby as the container for his anxiety was at the root of almost all of their fights. It would normally play out in the following way:

- Abbie and Drew would make a plan to do something

- The two of them would agree upon a time to leave

- Drew would start texting Abbie every couple minutes

- Drew would ask Abbie about what he was planning to wear

- Drew would wonder which freeway would have the most traffic

- Drew would update her about something he needed to take care of before leaving

- Drew would fill her in on how many amazing reviews the restaurant had received

- Drew would send her several funny memes he'd seen while scrolling on Instagram

- Drew would ask if he should stop to get some ice cream for them for after dinner

- Drew would arrive at Abbie's house twenty minutes after the time they'd discussed, finding a flustered, "hangry" Abbie

In the situation like the one described above, both Drew and Abbie would feel confused about what Drew had done to make Abbie so irritated. On the surface, it would seem that she was upset about his tardiness. But in reality, her irritation started long before Drew even arrived at the house. With every text she received, she could feel him pulling on her energetic resources more and more. Drew was not attuned to Abbie because he was so preoccupied with his own overwhelming emotions. He was looking to her for approval, assurance, validation, clarity—ultimately, he was looking for her to lead. Abbie could feel the energetic pull of his insecurity and the weight of the responsibility she felt to make him feel reassured and contained.

Many would say that it's unreasonable to expect that our partner (regardless of gender) will not expose us to the experience of their anxiety. And yes, of course that's true. But in this case, Drew hadn't gathered the emotional awareness to even know that he was moving through his life in a constant state of overwhelm, and looking for an external source of safety to contain him. This energetic pull from Drew caused Abbie to feel something maternal toward him that wasn't there when they first met. It reminded her of all the years she spent caring for her ex-husband without him having any regard for how his lack of emotional awareness was impacting her.

Society teaches men that they bear no responsibility in cultivating their own set of tools for nervous systems regulation—and in fact, they have been so shamed for their inability to do so that they're unwilling to even acknowledge it as an issue. So they either bottle it up, act it out in maladaptive ways, or create a sort of energetic leakage on the women in their lives. They've been taught that a woman's role is to be pleasing, to nurture, to soothe, and keep their external world light. If she gets upset, and challenges a man to take responsibility for himself, she is a scary bitch, and he is suddenly victimized by her irrational mood swings.

What I started to understand about Abbie's dynamic with both of these men was that she was experiencing a fundamental lack of masculine containment. This is where I think a lot of people who discuss masculine and feminine polarity misunderstand what a woman is longing for in terms of masculine leadership. I also find that many of my male clients struggle in the beginning with how to course correct when moving from a passive relational stance to the space of leadership.

A woman longing for masculine leadership is really not about her wanting a man to tell her what to do (and in most cases, he will be met with a great deal of resistance if he tries). A core feminine woman wants to feel the energetic sense that a man could protect her from the world, but **not from herself**. The minute a man attempts to protect a woman from herself, he becomes dad. Knowing what's best for you is paternal energy.

At the same time, embodying this passive energy while allowing himself to be led begins to cultivate a sense of resentment in a core masculine man over time. A man longs for woman to be nurturing, but not **in control of him**. Once she alludes to the fact that he is inept without her guidance, she begins to take on a maternal energy. Masculine leadership is really about a man knowing himself well enough that he is not looking for someone else to take on a leadership role in *his* life.

Healthy masculine energy is about having a clear mission and loving a challenge. It's the embodiment of self-awareness and confidence. It's having done enough inner work to know yourself well. It's having a set of tools in your toolkit to self-soothe through emotional turbulence. No matter how kind and loving a man presents himself as to a core feminine woman, if he is consistently looking for her to provide him with direction, over time she will resent him for it. She is looking for him to take responsibility for his own life.

This is one of the most challenging dynamics I see playing out with couples. Because on the surface, it doesn't feel fair. But this is one of the ways that attempting to create equality by pretending that there are no differences between men and women has done us a disservice. Some of this has to do with how we are socialized, but some of it has to do with the difference in what causes a state of authentic arousal for a core masculine vs. core feminine. And until it is said, explored, and acknowledged, it will inevitably create a state of relational conflict.

The point of unearthing this practice of harvesting feminine energy is not about shaming or blaming men. It's to point out that there are certain gender dynamics that society has not prepared us to consider. And it's not as though men benefit from this lack of emotional awareness. They either find themselves in a constant state of struggle with their partners, or unable to experience a rooted sense of self-confidence. We've been taught that emotional intimacy looks like each partner releasing difficult feelings onto the other without working to cultivate a sense of self-awareness, or considering the other person's capacity to hold what we are bringing to them. This is where we miss the opportunity to see our relational struggles as an invitation to come into a deeper understanding of ourselves.

Divine Masculine Leadership

Masculinity is not toxic. Patriarchal masculinity might be considered toxic. Uninitiated masculinity certainly can be. Distorted masculinity is at the root of everything that has corrupted, diminished, and oppressed the entire ecosystem we are inhabiting. But these energetics are all fundamentally in opposition to the essence of masculinity. In my opinion, our society has not suffered because of an abundance of masculine values, but because of the collective minimization of the quest for meaning that represents what masculinity is at its core. In his book *Man's Search for Meaning*, Austrian psychologist and Holocaust survivor Viktor Frankl states, "What man actually needs is not a tensionless state, but rather the striving and struggling for some goal worthy of him. What he needs is not the discharge of tension at any cost, but the call of a potential meaning waiting to be fulfilled by him."[2]

The human necessity for meaning can be traced back to the most fundamental questions of our human existence. How did we get here? What happens when we leave these bodies? And what is the meaning of life? These are the essential questions human animals have been seeking the answers to since the beginning of their arrival. The quest for the answers to these questions is at the center of all of our mental health struggles—the suffering that comes with loss, the anxiety about the future, the remorse we feel about mistakes from the past, and the most essential human fear: the fear of annihilation.

In a society that normalized and understood the value of making space for the fundamental human need to explore these questions, we would prioritize things like philosophy, the arts, and fellowship centered around this type of existential exploration. To a certain extent, this is what communities have historically found within the containment of religious organizations. The trouble with utilizing religious organizations as the sole arbiter of our existential truths is twofold: One, this requires a buy-in to a collective understanding of truth—and since truth can have as many interpretations as there are interpreters, this has generally been the source of some our greatest moments of human conflict. And two, because these religious organizations are run by human beings, this leaves those looking to their church for interpretation vulnerable to the indulgences, corruptions, and pain points of church leaders. Historical moments of realizing that the church was indeed vulnerable to corruption challenged our society to seek its answers to existential questions elsewhere.

This is where science, technology, and the search for what could be proven as tangible evidence stepped into the ring. This was the point where we decided to put our efforts into understanding our fundamental questions from a scientific perspective, and that perhaps building a life of comfort and security would offer us more value than the search for deeper meaning ever could. So, we put our faith in what could be proven and measured. We placed our hopes in the accumulation of power, status, and the creature comforts of a civilized world. This is where we traded in authentic aliveness for an illusionary sense of certainty—a wounded masculine paradigm as the status quo.

But in order for a society to submit to wounded masculine values like hyper-productivity, competition, the devaluation of emotions, and a lack of presence, it becomes necessary to disregard the most grounded, essential aspects of what makes authentic masculinity so sacred. Authentic masculinity is rooted in the depths of awareness that come from hard-fought battles. It is the unshakable self-confidence that can only come from initiatory tests. What has created a lack of masculine integrity is not the distinction of having more testosterone or a more challenging time tapping into emotional intelligence. This is the lie that patriarchy has sold all of us about masculinity. The truth is, it's the seeking of external validation instead of allowing one's life to be led by an inner authority that has led to the distortion of masculine energy that permeates our society today.

A capitalist society is strengthened by a lack of emotional maturity. Consumerism requires that we live in a perpetual state of believing we are not enough. The striving for a better car, a bigger house, designer jeans, the most prestigious schools, the fanciest vacation locales—these badges of consumerism all epitomize the collective brainwashing we're indoctrinated with early on. We're taught that once we achieve something external that represents a certain level of status, *then* we will be worthy of the acceptance, respect, and love that we desire. This will mean that we have done something "meaningful" with our lives. Except, those who reach the pinnacle of these societal status symbols often experience the most emotional suffering. Because once we attain what we're taught will bring us a sense of fulfillment and still feel unfulfilled, we are confronted with the same existential questioning we began with—only now with nothing left to strive for as a distraction.

The irony of a society that prioritizes the accumulation of material goods like cars, toys, external praise, and status in an attempt to be recognized as holding worth is that these values originate from an extremely wounded feminine energetic collectively. The wounded feminine looks for something outside of the self to cultivate self-worth. This is the energy of desperation, of inauthenticity—the energy that chases and believes that something external will make it whole. Yes, a patriarchal society attempts to reconcile these fears from a wounded masculine space, because the feminine energetic of emotions motivates us into the masculine energetic of action, but the core motivation driving this behavior is the collective shadow of our distorted relationship with the feminine. And this makes sense, because any aspect of our human psyche that we attempt to repress without first acknowledging its existence and attempting to understand it becomes the maladaptive aspects of who we are, holding us back from living a fully embodied existence.

The masculine aspects of who we are (the physical body) require the feminine aspects of who we are (the Soul) to cultivate a sense of meaning. Without a sense of meaning, we remain stuck in a perpetual adolescent state—chasing empty pleasures, obsessing over meaningless distractions, and looking to the external world to affirm us like a simulated father figure. This unintegrated masculine energy is the feeling of stagnation. It's the space we inhabit until we make the decision to brave the wilderness and encounter our deepest fears.

At one point, this was a developmental aspect of the initiation process, ushering adolescent boys into manhood. Elders would support them through the same rituals they themselves had faced. This is how they were guided toward the path of the warrior—aiding them in facing their fears, and coming out on the other side with an embodied sense of who they were and what they were capable of. We are alchemized into the space of our becoming by the moments we imagine might destroy us. Unfortunately, we are a society that no longer recognizes this. We dismiss the inherent value in any sort of discomfort, in seeking wisdom from our elders, making time for rites of passage, prioritizing grounded leadership, or teaching our youth that they have everything required for survival within the boundaries of their own skin.

The energetic of the Divine Masculine is the remembrance of this metaphorical path of the warrior. This is the departure from the creature comforts of our delusions to the confrontation of our psyche's greatest fears. It's the rumble with death that crystalizes our understanding of who we are and what matters most to us. This is a quest few undertake in our modern society. And while this disengagement from our healthy masculine essence impacts all of us, it has been especially detrimental to men with a masculine core. Their fathers, and their father's fathers, have forgotten the beauty of the distinct aspects of their own masculine nature. This has had a tremendous impact not only on their relationships, but ultimately on the way they feel about themselves.

We are living amongst a society of men who have been forced to sever the veracity of their humanity in exchange for the promise of a sense of belonging. Incidentally, it's a sense of belonging amongst those who are just as lost as they are. This perpetual state of striving to "become something" has left today's men feeling lost and hollow, with no real sense of meaning. Nothing they'll have to exhale into when their lives are said and done. Men cannot be leaders in their careers, their homes, or their communities if they have no sense of how to take the lead in their own lives. Because ultimately, this requires that they cease looking to the world around them to define what it means to be a man, and begin the long journey inward to defining this for themselves.

CHAPTER 9

Reclaiming the Feminine

*"until a woman can receive herself, she will unconsciously
force others to reject her, despite the fact that
her most conscious desire is to be loved."*

MARION WOODMAN

"Perfect" Armor

first things first. We have to go back for her. When the ground beneath our feet has finally eroded. When we've been violated and disregarded in unspeakable ways. When the marriage and family we've been defined by has evaporated. When we look in the mirror and can't even recognize the woman we've become. When something enters our life that makes us want to stop playing small and fight for our own sense of aliveness. When we realize the only person that we will always be able to count on is ourself. When we've finally reached our breaking point, and we're sick and tired of being sick and tired. We have to go back for the little girl we left behind.

She was taught that her only hope of survival was diminishment. She gathered countless bits of evidence that supported her trepidations about being a girl in this world. She was deceived into believing that her super-powers were liabilities. She is furious. Heartbroken. Cynical. Exhausted. She just wants to be left alone. So you have to go back for her.

A society that rejects every part of the feminine teaches little girls to carry the weight of a deep-seated disdain for their essence. Disdain for their uncontrollable bodies. Disdain for their desire to be seen and loved.

Disdain for their longing to roam freely without the fear of judgment or injury. Disdain for their dark, wild, uninhibited feminine magic.

Her magic carries within it the greatest threat to patriarchal order and the ruling status quo. It is a questioning of what lies beyond the "civilized world" as we've known it, and the possibility of experiencing something more. Her magic holds the power to manifest life. The force that creates entire stratospheres. Her womb is the sacred portal to the recognized awareness that we are eternal beings.

Everything about what the feminine essence is represents a connection to the ethereal forces that reside within us. These powers are not meant to be understood or contained. But if you are going to dominate and create fear within an entire society, the power that the feminine energetic holds must be dismissed, erased, and ultimately, controlled.

Alice Walker said, "The most common way people give up their power is by thinking they don't have any."[1] Patriarchal systems have utilized a form of psychological warfare to convince women of their powerlessness for thousands of years. Elements of this warfare have included:

1. persuading them that their only power lies in their ability to make themselves into appealing objects

2. teaching them to source their sense of belonging from keeping up with rigid standards of beauty

3. convincing them that the only acceptable path to fulfillment is by taking on specific roles, like wife and mother

4. collectively shaming, minimizing, and discarding feminine qualities like creativity, sensuality, and vulnerability

5. conditioning them to believe that their instinctual feminine desires to be loved and seen are needy and weak

The desire within all of us to feel our interconnectedness is an intrinsically feminine quality. Convincing human beings that the longing to feel unconditionally safe, seen, and supported by one another equates to a form of weakness is the ultimate weaponization of our fundamental human need for attachment. This form of psychological indoctrination begins early, and is only one aspect of how all of us—but especially women—are trained to forget where our power lies.

Women are conditioned to dissect and identify with their exterior (a masculine characteristic) instead of spending their time cultivating a rich and trusting relationship with their intuition and inner world (a feminine characteristic). They are taught to compare themselves to, minimize, and compete with other women (wounded masculine characteristics) instead of leaning into collaboration, a belief in abundance, and trusting what is meant for each of us will always materialize in Divine timing (healthy feminine characteristics). Women are conditioned to view feminine sensuality as dangerous, deceptive, and untrustworthy. They're taught that when a woman is sexually assaulted by a man who physically overpowers her, he was in some way victimized by her sensual prowess—or that her behavior, attire, or intentions should be what is questioned, instead of his disconnection from his own humanity. Women are trained to view their need to connect and their emotionality as unproductive and burdensome, causing them to suppress their desire for deep intimacy in exchange for what fits neatly in a societal box.

These acts of psychological warfare are the training that strips women of their authenticity. We are conditioned to believe that our messy, uncontained, fully alive, authentic selves are fundamentally unlovable. Because more than any other thing that women are taught, we teach women that those who are worthy of love are perfect. Perfect bodies, perfect mothers, perfect home lives, perfect social calendars, perfect work/life balance, perfectly satisfied partners, perfect pictures of perfect vacations on perfectly curated social outlets. Women are not meant to be human. They are meant to be perfect, perfect, perfect. Just as men are taught that they earn societal belonging through their ability to be stoic, women are taught that their sense of societal belonging is earned through their ability to be perfect.

But we are not perfect. Our bodies require sustenance, which interferes with our ability to seamlessly keep them fitting into perfect sizes. Our children are unruly humans, which interferes with our ability to keep them behaving like perfect little robots. Our work life competes with our home life, which makes it a struggle to perfectly balance how we show up in each arena. Our social obligations and to-do lists feel never-ending, causing a perfect state of internal overwhelm that we're constantly attempting to suppress. And our partners start to feel like just another part of this whole damn system, making them the perfect villains to project our frustrations upon. I have sat with countless women describing the frustration they feel, helplessly attempting to juggle all of these variables and unable to understand why they feel a low-level discontent with their entire lives. The feeling that there is something wrong with them, and their inability to achieve perfection, leaves many women feeling isolated and defective.

The female quest for perfection manifests in a variety of ways. It shows up in the desire to control our exterior—our bodies, our beauty routines, and our aging process. It shows up in our codependent relationships with others—our fixing and people pleasing tendencies, our affinity for manipulation, and the minimization of our needs, followed by overwhelming sensations of resentment. It can also show up in the constant undulation between the dichotomies of the belief that we are too much or never enough. Our constant need to be productive, but believing that there is always someone, somewhere doing it better. The visceral disgust we feel toward those who are "full of themselves," as we constantly strive to be worthy of being seen. And our disjointed belief that we have a clear idea of what others should do, while living in a constant state of questioning ourselves. The idea that there is a "perfect" way to do life, and living in a perpetual state of striving to achieve it, is the wounded masculine armor women have been conditioned to believe will keep us safe.

I remember my first moment of being confronted with my own attempts to manage internalized ideas about perfection. I understand now that these attempts are why I felt such a deep sense of liberation when I first started getting stoned. Pot offered me a form of relief from the protective armor I wore of attempting to be perfect. When I was young, I thought I needed to be the perfect minority to combat negative stereotypes people held about women of color. As I got older, I attempted to look perfect. I was taught (and received feedback that confirmed) that meeting a societal standard of what was considered acceptable meant figuring out how to fit in with the other girls and garner attention from the boys at school. This did not come without a fair amount of effort. As I aged, the rigid standards of what society deems an acceptable body weight for an attractive woman felt more and more difficult to maintain. I would find myself obsessively worried about whether or not I was being perceived as attractive by others, instead of being fully present in my interactions with them.

Pot offered me a sense of relief from this constant state of striving. Suddenly I had a tangible cloak to wrap around myself as I explored the boundaries of my internal world uninterrupted. It offered me the felt sense that how other people perceived me was completely irrelevant. I didn't care. This was the protective armor that I had been longing to wear for a lifetime. Suddenly I felt safe enough to be in my body, lighthearted and playful, bold and creative, introspective and curious, sexually free and uninhibited, connected to my Soul space, and inspired. It wasn't until years later that I realized it—what pot had given me was access to my feminine. It showed me how to reconnect to a vital aspect of myself in a way that I'd been taught to shut down when I was a little girl.

But the thing about wearing a cloak of armor around you is that it can be extremely difficult to give and receive love. We can't fully engage in all of the most sacred moments of our human experience if we need something outside of ourselves to give us access to who we truly are. Carl Jung once wrote in a letter to Bill W. (the founder of Alcoholics Anonymous) that he believed that those struggling with an addiction to alcohol were seeking a connection to their own Divinity. He said, "Craving for alcohol was the equivalent on a low level of the spiritual thirst of our being for wholeness, expressed in medieval language: the union with God."[2] In the beginning, any "spirit" like drugs and alcohol can feel like a gateway to access transcendent states of reality. But if we get lost in the need for something outside of ourselves to feel a connection to our Soul space, we can lose sight of what we came into this life to achieve.

All of our addictive tendencies become a way to armor ourselves against the pain of what feels unbearable to face. But if we come to the recognition that we have lost ourselves in the protective armor of an addiction, it can be an invitation to a larger inquiry about how we truly feel about the life we are attempting to escape. For so many women, addictive tendencies show up as a means to cope with the excruciating pressure we are under to be perfect in a world where we know we are set up to fail. There will always be someone thinner, younger, prettier, more successful, with better behaved children, taking more exotic vacations, with a partner who adores her, and seemingly doing it all with ease, making us feel like whatever we're doing is just not good enough.

Unless. Unless we decide we don't want to play a game that we can't win anymore. Putting down our armor in search of what it means to reclaim our feminine is the equivalent of picking up our ball and making the decision to head home.

Rediscovering the Soul

The thing about letting go of whatever we've been attempting to control is that there's always an exhale—a questioning of why we didn't just let go of this sooner. Because the truth is, there's an element of what we find when we finally start to take off our armor that each of us have been so unbelievably hungry to reclaim. This is the space of trusting in our ability to show up authentically. To live a life that feels grounded in a sense of connection and aliveness. To break out of the self-imposed cages we've been conditioned to live in. These cages, which are made up of manufactured ideas of what our lives "should" be and look like, are the ultimate rejection of the feminine wisdom that resides within us. The emancipation from these cages is the remembrance of our Soul wisdom—and ultimately, the remembrance of the person we came into these bodies to be. Because the larger truth that modern society supports us in overlooking is that when we get to the end of our time here, we will find that most of our daily concerns were irrelevant. The amount of pleasure, connection, expansion, and love we experienced while we were here, however, is what will carry on.

And so the question becomes: how do we consistently embody the energetic of our Soul space and reclaim the feminine aspects of who we are? The difficult truth is that most of us don't get there without a fight. Our ego will defend vehemently against surrendering to this level of aliveness. Because trusting in the infinite wisdom of life's natural unfolding requires a series of ego deaths to dispel the illusion that the ego was ever working in support of our highest Self. The ego is not interested in us having this level of awakening. But in the words of mythopoetic author Marion Woodman, "What the ego wants is tiny compared to what the Soul wants, and there comes a point when we recognize this, and we surrender to Soul."[3]

Millie and Lauren had been married for almost four years, together for nine, when they came in to do some couples work. Up until the eighth year of their relationship, things between them had been pretty copasetic—certainly not void of any difficulty, but for the most part they knew how to navigate challenges well and had a healthy level of love and respect for one another. Over the last year, however, they had been confronted with difficulties that started to bring everything about their relationship into question. They had both experienced a significant amount of loss in a very short amount of time—suddenly losing best friends, aspects of their jobs, and family members, all in the midst of a global pandemic that shifted the way the entire world had been functioning up to this point. This suddenly put their relationship in what felt like an extremely destabilized place.

Before the series of losses they'd suffered, Millie would have considered herself to be the core masculine in their dynamic. Millie was driven, loved to compete, wasn't necessarily one for sitting and deeply processing feelings, and before she met Lauren, often labeled herself as avoidant due to her resistance to being tied down to one relationship. Lauren, however, would have been seen by most as the core feminine in their dynamic. Lauren often looked to Millie for a sense of emotional safety and for affirmation of the love she felt for her. She often overcompensated for her insecurities with a propensity toward people pleasing, and in the last year, with so much loss to reconcile in her mind, was clinging to their relationship in a way that felt alarming and a bit overwhelming to Millie. The truth was, each of them had been shaken to their core. Their entire conceptualization of safety and significance had been shattered by the visceral reality of experiencing so much loss in such a short amount of time.

What I started to recognize as I worked with Millie and Lauren was that what we might've perceived to be their core energetics on the surface weren't in alignment with the truth of what they needed to heal on a Soul level. Here's what I mean:

Millie had shown up as the more core masculine energetic throughout the entirety of their relationship. But what I started to realize about her masculine energy was that it was being driven by a very wounded space within her. It was the energy of never feeling good enough. Constantly feeling the need to overcompensate for the ways that she'd felt judged and rejected. Her masculine energy wasn't providing a rooted sense of containment and leadership in her dynamic with Lauren. It was filled with resentment and contempt for the sense of burden and responsibility she felt was being placed upon her.

Lauren, however, was embodying a wounded feminine energetic in her relationship with Millie. She was essentially making her relationship her primary coping mechanism to compensate for the lack of safety she felt in all other facets of life. She was perpetuating the belief in their dynamic (as she had in all of her relationships) that she was simply too much for anyone to tolerate or truly be able to love. Holding this fear created a dynamic that almost became a self-fulfilling prophecy for Lauren. The more desperately she attempted to cling to Millie, the more she seemed to push her away.

What was so beautiful about this relational challenge between Millie and Lauren was that it perfectly activated each of their core wounds in a way that was impossible for them to deny. Millie had developed the survival mechanism of avoidance in an attempt to defend against the rejection she felt in her family of origin. As a gay woman, she felt completely rejected by a mother who struggled to understand her. Her avoidance created a protective barrier around her of never allowing herself to "need" anyone again. Lauren, however, had cultivated the opposite coping mechanism in a family where she felt desperate to have someone—anyone—pay attention to her. Her divorced parents had been so consumed with their own struggles (namely, their competing needs to be better than the other parent) that she often felt a sense of desperation for someone to see her there and acknowledge the fact that she had needs at all.

Loss can frequently become the stimulus that ushers us back into a more authentic way of living. The shadow elements of what both Millie and Lauren were feeling for the other were the precise elements of themselves that each of them needed to reclaim. The overwhelming feeling of responsibility that Lauren's needs brought up in Millie was the precise feeling she'd experienced from her mother. The suffocation she felt when Lauren was being too needy was the irritation she was harboring toward the abandoned child within her—the child who felt her mother's overwhelm and shamed herself for needing the unconditional warmth and acceptance of a mother's love. She was projecting onto Lauren the anger she felt toward herself. She was projecting outward what felt intolerable to acknowledge and hold compassionately within herself.

As for Lauren, her propensity to make another person her Higher Power was the continuance of what the little girl within her had needed from her parents—as a little girl, she wasn't able to see them as flawed humans, struggling with their own insecurities, pain points, and sensations of overwhelm but as omnipresent forces that for some reason were withholding their parental duties of mirroring back to her a sense of worth and belonging. The story she told herself when she felt rejected by her parents as a child was that she must be fundamentally unlovable. Her subconscious was recreating this dynamic, hoping to cultivate a different outcome in adulthood. This caused her to choose partners who felt overwhelmed by another person's desire for love and connection. This dynamic perpetuated Lauren's false belief that she was fundamentally unlovable.

After the losses that Lauren and Millie experienced, they had a visceral need to address what each of them had been able to keep just below the surface up to that point. The sense of destabilization they were each experiencing internally shifted their previous survival mechanisms into overdrive. Millie shifted into hyper-wounded masculine energy, Lauren into hyper-wounded feminine energy. This could've conceivably pushed them so far apart from one another that they might have been unable to find their way back. Instead, we practiced seeing what was activated within each of them as a profound invitation from the Universe to heal.

Millie was able to gradually explore who she would be if she didn't feel like she had so much to prove, if she gave herself space to grieve on behalf of the little girl within her that had desperately longed for unconditional acceptance and love from her mother. She began to see that there was a force much larger than any human (and their human challenges) that had loved her, believed in her, and been right there with her on every step of her journey up to this point. This was the reclamation of her relationship to the Source energy within her. And what we found on the other side of that reclamation was that Millie had been suppressing a lot more core feminine energy than she could have possibly imagined. She felt an overwhelming sense of liberation in the realization that ultimately, what she was most hungry for was the ability to soften, play, and trust that everything would work out in Divine order.

Lauren's reclamation was about tapping into an ability to see herself more clearly. By processing her parents' human limitations through the eyes of an adult, she was able to validate the innate worth of her inner child in a way that she'd never been able to see before. As she started to understand the process of individuation, she began embodying an emotional maturity that allowed her to see her parents as two people who simply didn't have the tools to navigate their way through the turbulent waters of heartbreak. Not only was she able to empathize with the feeling of overwhelm they must've been experiencing at the time, but validate how some of her own emotional resilience and adaptability had been cultivated by growing up in each of their homes. This increased her capacity to expand her vision of Millie beyond believing her to be the source of her salvation and the person responsible for her caretaking. She was able to care for herself. This gave her the ability to hold a much more present, healthy masculine energetic within their partnership.

There is power in reclaiming the way we hold our most difficult moments. Instead of seeing them as horrific events that never should have happened, we can work to view them as initiatory periods, guiding us back home to a more authentic version of who we are. A wounded masculine relationship paradigm teaches us to view the dynamic between Lauren and Milly through the lens of what needs to be "fixed" about their behavior patterns or methods of communicating. If we make the sole focus how each of them could more effectively empathize with the other's experience, we miss the larger synchronistic unfolding of why each of them are offering the other a perfect container for what they need to heal. Wounded masculine strategies for tackling relationship struggles often miss the sacred nature of what is happening between two people in conflict. But the healthy feminine perspective holds that each of them are being birthed into the next iteration of who they are meant to become. The feminine principle maintains that everything we experience in our lifetime is in service to the greater blossoming of our potential, our ability to cultivate authentic connections, and the remembrance of who we truly are.

Held and Free

There is a dichotomy that exists within the heart of the feminine. This is true of the feminine essence within all of us, but rings especially true in the hearts of women who have been socialized to adhere to certain expectations, restraints, ideals, and survival mechanisms that have shaped our perception of ourselves and who we are in relationship to others. This dichotomy is the desire to feel both held and free in relationship. This is something that I've heard author Glennon Doyle frequently speak about in her own journey to find fulfillment in relationships. In her book *Untamed*, she also mentions the concept of a relationship where you can feel both "held and free."[4] The first time I heard her say it, I thought to myself—*that.* That is the longing that I could never quite articulate or understand wanting to feel in the midst of my own marriage, and what I witness so many women grappling to understand within themselves. But before we can even begin to negotiate how to cultivate this experience relationally, we have to understand what is at the heart of this longing within ourselves.

So we begin with the untamed healthy energetic of the feminine—this is the energy within us that is ever-shifting, moment to moment. Intuitive, emotional, messy. The part of us that meets each moment with an innate curiosity about what could be brimming just beneath the surface of what is shown. The feminine represents the first inkling of what will be birthed into physical form from the Source of creation. It's the vision, the feeling, the knowing. The feminine energetic thrives when the innate wisdom of its cycles of manifestation are seen, revered, and honored for what they are.

But in order for any of us to tap into this level of intuitive wisdom, we require a foundation of safety off of which we can feel free to launch. This is the acknowledgment of the "roots and wings" principle within our human development. We need a launchpad in order to launch. A runway to gain enough momentum to fly. A sense of stability in our lives before we can be present with a true sense of aliveness. We need a healthy masculine structure before we can feel safe enough to receive from the space of our feminine.

The sexual interplay cultivated between a core masculine and a core feminine can be a beautiful illustration of healthy chemistry between polarities. The anatomical makeup of the masculine is the stable structure that enters the feminine. What creates an arousal state within the feminine is the experience of being seen, desired, and ultimately pursued. In order for the feminine to feel safe enough to lose herself in the internal sensations, the reckless sense of abandon, and the powerful transcendent moments that are the physical embodiment of the shared life force between the two energetics, she must believe that the masculine can support her in the midst of the unknown. The masculine, in accordance with this dance, is aroused by the depth of the feminine's trust. Her willingness to surrender into his capable containment is the tangible experience of what it means to penetrate the sacred nature of life force in its essence.

But our society has devalued the sacred nature of our relationship to sex, in the same way that it has devalued the feminine. We've deemed it empowering to have casual sex based solely on a longing for external validation, turned sex into another thing on our to-do lists regardless of what we truly desire, and intertwined our sex lives with feelings of shame, virtue signaling, or something that should be reserved for the purpose of procreation. The mixed signals we're conditioned to internalize about one of the most organic, tender, pleasurable expressions of the felt experience of our aliveness have hijacked the sacred nature of sex and turned it into another relational pain point we're in a constant state of negotiating. This is a wounded masculine interpretation of a healthy feminine expression of our humanity. Instead of the meeting of two Souls who come together in physical form to play, create, heal, and transcend, sex has become a tool for deeper numbing, dominating, controlling, withholding, and frankly, cultivating further injury.

For women especially, reclaiming the feminine aspects of ourselves that have been appropriated by a wounded masculine culture requires a radical form of softening. But taking off the rigid layers of masculine armor we've spent a lifetime positioning around ourselves can be easier said than done. It requires a level of trust and uncompromising surrender that our entire nervous system has been programmed to defend against. Every part of us wants to resist making ourselves vulnerable to others. We often feel a sickening sense of contempt and embarrassment when an uncontrollable longing comes over us to be held and cherished. We instinctually deem ourselves weak, naïve, or pitiful anytime we find ourselves on the receiving end of a broken heart. I'd be lying if I didn't admit that I still catch myself struggling not to judge myself or other women as being "too needy" when they dare to have any relational needs at all. And given how unbelievably taxing it can feel to put down our swords and dare to leave our hearts open to obliteration, we might ask ourselves: why in the world would we make the choice to soften in the first place? Because every single aspect of the truest parts of who we are is desperately longing to do just that.

This is another one of those truths that it can be difficult to convince someone of until they've experienced it within themselves. Although, I do believe that some part of us knows this on an intuitive level. The part of us that knows we are living out of alignment with our Souls' deepest longings lives with a low-level bitterness that we struggle to understand. As a core feminine, we can have a partner who is unbelievably kind, shows up without question, desperately attempts to meet our needs, and is unwavering in their loyalty, and we will often feel an ineffable sense of contempt toward them that we feel baffled by. This is for the same reason you often hear people say that women are less attracted to "nice guys." It's because for a core feminine woman, her deepest longing is to be held in the presence of a masculine energy that is strong enough to allow her to release control.

The untamed nature of the feminine essence will instinctually test the masculine presence, surveying his behavior to see, "Do you have a strong enough backbone to stand your ground with me? Can you embody a solid sense of who you are regardless of the fluctuations I may throw your way?" This testing is not a conscious decision she makes; it stems from a primal necessity to cultivate safety for herself and possibly her offspring. But if she senses that there is an unsteadiness in the masculine before her, she will feel compelled to create that safety for herself. And she will resent the hell out of him for it.

I want to be very clear that there was a time not long ago when EVERY. PART. OF. ME. would have scoffed at the idea of a feminine desire to surrender fully into the safety of masculine containment. Until I had the felt experience of being able to do so for the first time. It was like the remembrance of some part of me that had been dormant for so long, I didn't even realize it was there. It was the experience of feeling contained in an environment that felt clear and steady enough for me to remember and unleash an aspect of my feminine wild. And honestly, this interplay goes on in modern mating rituals all the time. It's just that these energetics are often distorted and cultivated in a way that perpetuates our wounds. The dance of the more avoidant attachment style (wounded masculine energy) that withholds affection in an attempt to bring forward a sense of desperation (wounded feminine energy) is an example of how polarity can instinctually be used (regardless of a person's gender) to manipulate a sense of desire.

But manipulated desire is not authentic connection. It doesn't satiate our Souls' deepest longings in the way that a core feminine is capable of experiencing when she is held by unwavering masculine stability. Sure, runner/chaser dynamics may offer a momentary taste of a transcendent hit of ecstasy in the same way that a momentary euphoria is experienced by someone addicted to heroin. But a relational experience that offers healing and a sense of Soul alignment cannot be sourced from an internal deficit that we're attempting to compensate for. There will always be an undertone of anxiety that creates a barrier to intimacy. The need to self-protect will show up in various forms of unconscious sabotage. This is what prevents us from allowing ourselves to feel held and free in relationships—a lack of trust. Softening into resolute trust is an essential aspect of healing for the feminine. But as long as our ability to trust is dependent on an external masculine source, it will show up in an inauthentic way. It will believe that it requires being seen by that masculine source to feel a sense of wholeness. And because on a Soul level we know this isn't true, our Soul will not let us rest in inauthentic power.

Feeling safe enough to fully soften into authentic feminine power must begin with the integration of our internal masculine energy. All of the elements of what the core feminine is longing to experience from an external masculine source already exist within. Recognizing our ability to set clear boundaries and act as our own fierce protector, our ability to see our own Divinity and celebrate our gifts, and our ability to hold reverent space for every aspect of our feminine essence (our creation, our emotions, our sensuality, our messiness, our fire, our radiance, our darkness and light, our wild untamed exuberance, our intuition, and our ability to receive) is how we integrate a solid sense of our own internal masculine. The reclaiming of our inner feminine from a world that taught us to turn away from ourselves lies in our ability to hold and safeguard our own feminine complexity while granting ourselves the freedom to embody the fullest expression of ourselves in absolute awe and wonder.

Divine Feminine Leadership

One day I was sitting in a café and writing when a man and a woman came in and sat down at the table right next to me. The man was considerably older, appearing to be in his late forties, and the younger woman in her early twenties. She was dressed for a business meeting—full suit, heels, and a briefcase under her arm. The man, on the other hand, was casually dressed in grey sweats and sneakers. Now, I'm not actually the type of person that does a lot of eavesdropping on other people's conversations. But on this day, I had forgotten my headphones and the man was speaking very loudly, so I couldn't help but overhear their conversation. It quickly became clear to me that he was this young woman's client, and that they were having a business meeting to discuss the publicity for an event that she was planning for his company. I found myself feeling more and more agitated as I listened to the tone in which he was speaking to her. He was irritated that she had requested a clear description of his budget before continuing to secure vendors for his upcoming event.

"You're only like twenty years old, so you don't understand a lot about how to get these things done," he said. "I used to do this type of work—way back when I was your age, and it's all about scratching other people's backs. If you had any skills in doing this type of work, you would know how to call in some favors, offer vendors some exposure, and even figure out how to make a little extra on the back end. I'm trying to throw you a bone by giving you an opportunity, since you're clearly very new at this. But I'm not going to throw a bunch of money into this project for you to mess around with, when you haven't given me any indication of how resourceful you can be in calling in some favors."

Now aside from the fact that what he was saying to her struck me as being utterly ridiculous, I couldn't help but notice the energetic exchange happening between the two of them as he continued to speak. As he spoke, she began to contract—shrinking down lower into her chair. He would ask her questions and not allow her to reply. He would scoff and minimize aspects of her email request as he read them back to her. It was clear that he hadn't called this young woman into a public place for a business meeting to gain greater insight about what she was capable of offering his company, but rather to deliver a long-winded monologue about his vast experience and insight and to make her feel small. It was everything I could do to sit there silently without interjecting something on this young woman's behalf. What I wanted to say to her was "Run, sister. Run. Whatever this man might pay you for the work you're able to do for him, I promise you it will not be worth it."

But of course, I couldn't say that to her. I didn't know anything about her, her situation, or how much she might need to stay seated, tolerating this level of belittlement for a job that she had to do. There's nothing unique about this story. Women share these types of anecdotes with me about the narcissistic energy of those above them in workplace environments all the time. Those who feel more powerful and strong by seeking to make someone else feel weak. Those who dominate and control rather than collaborate and encourage. Those who believe in lack, aggression, minimization, and fear over the possibility of uplifting through the example they can set. Those who utilize the same wounded masculine energy that they themselves were harmed by to continue the cycle of harm as they become the perpetrators of harm to others. And this type of wounded masculine behavior is in no way exclusive to either gender. So much of what we have taught women to believe is required to succeed in the work force is to emulate the patriarchal status quo.

But I couldn't help but wonder as I sat there how different that experience might have been for that young woman if she had been sitting with an elder—regardless of their gender—who was willing to approach that conversation with an integrated sense of healthy feminine energy. If the same man had been curious about her conclusions and open to what he might be missing. If he had been humble enough to be vulnerable with his concerns about excessive costs. If he'd been open to the fun they might tap into if they collaborated on creative ways to save money together. If he'd allowed himself to be human with her, instead of armoring up with righteousness and false bravado. He could have modeled a sense of what leadership looks like to someone at an impressionable point in her career. Instead, best-case scenario, he made himself into the memory of a challenging client who modeled to this woman everything not to be, do, and become in her own career; or worst-case scenario, he caused her to internalize the short-sighted beliefs he was projecting onto her in a way that was (more than likely) done to him.

Roy T. Bennett said, "Great leaders create more leaders, not followers. Great leaders have vision, share vision, and inspire others to create their own."[5] This is a standard of leadership rooted in the feminine principle. Leadership that looks beyond how I will be impacted by the decisions I make in this moment and looks toward the type of world I want to live in and create for my children. The first stages of the feminist movement—focused on equal rights, protection, and moving the needle toward the acknowledgment of a woman's shared humanity—were crucial, and have provided benefits for women of my generation beyond what can possibly be expressed. But the next stage of feminism requires a larger vision, one that encapsulates the reclamation and celebration of the feminine aspects of each and every one of us.

I dream of my son living in a world where his feminine essence is held as sacred—first and foremost by himself, but then by society at large. Where he becomes the type of leader whose movement is based on what inspires him, not what makes him feel afraid. I hope that whoever he chooses to love, he will have the courage to stay curious and open to creating a love story based on what they decide together—not what society has decided for them. I hope that he will prioritize being a good steward of the earth that he is inhabiting—understanding that the way we treat the Source from which we came directly correlates to our relationship with ourselves. But mostly, I hope that he feels that his mother modeled healthy feminine leadership for him in our home. That I gave myself permission to be messy and dark, imperfect and worthy, brave while afraid, vulnerable and collaborative, radiant and heart-centered, trusting and receptive, and overwhelmed with gratitude for every single breath I was given while inhabiting this body.

CHAPTER 10

Sovereign Love

"love and the work of soul are inextricably entwined. the other
is not here to take care of our soul, but rather to enlarge our
experience of it. such a gift is most precious to the one enlarged."

JAMES HOLLIS

Needs vs. Desires

barbra Streisand wasn't exactly wrong when she sang, "People who need people are the luckiest people in the world."[1] I understand the larger implication of the sentiment and wholeheartedly agree that isolation can be one of the most detrimental challenges the human psyche can face. We are pack animals—meant to bear witness to one another in community, support one another in the process of our expansion, and have shared expressions of love and connection that create meaning in our lives. *And*, the challenging conversation to have about where our pendulum has swung as a society is that we've become a bit obsessed with outsourcing our ability to navigate uncomfortable feelings to those around us. We've done this in an attempt to course correct the implications of being a "pull yourself up by your bootstraps" and "children should be seen and not heard" society. This course correction is completely understandable. But in our reaction to this avoidant form of wounded masculine isolationism, we've normalized an anxious form of wounded feminine enmeshment that—from my perspective—is stunting our relational growth in a completely different way.

The phrase *getting your needs met* has become such a common aspect of the cultural vernacular that it's rare to see a social media post about relationships that doesn't make reference to it in some way. People offer entire courses on how to effectively communicate your needs, bullet-pointed posts circulate about creating boundaries when your needs aren't getting met, and it's a rare couple that comes in for couples work without stating how and why they feel their needs are not being met by their partner.

Now please hear me clearly: **I am in no way saying we shouldn't have relational needs**. Of course we will, and we should. But when our ability to experience any kind of peace is dependent on another person's behavior, this is an outsourcing of our power. This is wounded feminine energy, and it is not sustainable. I have yet to meet anyone who created a significant behavioral change in their lives for any other reason than an authentic desire within themselves to do so. Certainly not because their partner desired that they change, or eventually nagged them into submission. But because they decide for themselves that a change needed to be made.

From my perspective, this is the origin point of most of our relational conflict: feeling like I need another person to "meet my needs" without really asking myself *why* this particular need is a need that I have. In my experience, there's always a wound unrelated to our partner that not having this need met reminds us of. There's always a way that we felt neglected, disregarded, unseen, or unloved in our past. The trouble is, in our attempt to feel loved and seen by our partners in the way that we didn't feel loved and seen when we were young, we end up behaving in some very unloving ways. In doing so, we end up pushing our partners away and recreating the feeling of abandonment we're unconsciously attempting to avoid. Our ego mind tells us a story in the moment about why our partner is consciously making the decision to disregard our needs—when in reality, they're not even consciously thinking about our needs, because they're caught up in their own mind with their own struggles.

Here's an example of what I mean, and this is a really common way this shows up for couples. Let's say for instance that my six-year-old son were to leave his clothes on the floor when he comes home and changes after school. This scenario is not much of a stretch to imagine for anyone who's a parent. When I see his clothes on the floor, I might roll my eyes, give him a gentle reminder about picking up his things, and make the assumption that in his excitement about whatever his next activity was, he forgot to put his clothes in the hamper. This is what is known as offering the *most generous interpretation* of his behavior. Quite often in our partnerships, however, the person who tends to be the over-functioner in the couple will describe a similar scenario with their partner leaving their socks or clothes on the floor, but their ego mind will swap in the *least generous interpretation* of their partner's behavior. They will tell themselves the story that their partner treats them like a maid or that they think it's their responsibility to do everything around the house. In other words, they take their partner's carelessness personally and feel overwhelmed with resentment.

Now before you even say it (and most people seem to have a very similar response to this analogy), **I'm not saying that your partner shouldn't be an adult who is responsible for picking up their own clothing**. What I'm saying is there are two important points here to consider:

1. Most of the time, a lack of ownership of these types of tasks didn't just happen overnight. People who tend to leave their clothing on the floor tend to be people who have historically left their clothing on the floor. Some of the work of finding peace around this issue is the personal responsibility we have to take for why this behavior pattern in our partner has suddenly become intolerable. In other words, we often put an extra emphasis on our partner's behavior as a way of sidestepping the decision we made to partner with a messy adult, believing that we could get them to change.

   But in the meantime, the personal inquiry becomes: What is the story I'm telling myself about what this means? Why am I taking this personally? Why do I assume my partner is doing this as a way of disregarding me, instead of assuming that they were distracted and not thinking about me at all— the same way I would assume was the case with a child?

2. There is subconscious aspect of the human psyche that will
   inevitably resist being controlled. This is the part of us
   that longs to be loved unconditionally. This part of us will
   resist—even subtly—any suggestion by someone else that we
   should be something other than who we are. This is why you
   can ask your partner to pick up their socks repeatedly and
   although they may do it for a week or two, they will often
   fall back into the unconscious pattern of resisting what you
   want them to do, because they do not want to be controlled.

I often use the example of socks as a point of contention between couples because it serves as a benign example of how we are more activated by the lack of consideration from our partner than we might be by someone else in our life. But then the question becomes: how do I negotiate my need to live in a clean house with my partner's unwillingness to pick up their socks?

This is where I think it can be much more productive to meet your partner in the space of vulnerability instead of attempting to control. Once you've done your own internal inquiry around why your partner leaving their socks on the floor feels so upsetting to you, you take the vulnerable step of sharing that information with your partner. This might sound something like: "Babe, you know how I'm always griping at you about leaving your socks on the floor? I was thinking about why it bothers me so much. What I realized is, it reminds me a lot of the way my mother made me responsible for cleaning up after my younger siblings because she was never home. When I see your socks on the floor, I tell myself the story that I'll always be responsible for taking care of everyone else."

We'll get into how to cultivate healthy polarity a bit more in the next section, but when you share with your partner from a space of vulnerability, you are shifting your energy from a wounded masculine energetic of control to a healthy feminine energetic of collaboration. This offers your partner the opportunity to meet you in a healthy masculine energetic of protection and containment. It's the distinction between your partner making a change in your relationship because they want to, versus it being demanded of them. This to me is what creates the distinction between a "need getting met" and "sharing why I desire what I desire" with my partner.

The distinction in how this scenario feels when we're talking about a child's behavior versus that of our adult partner tells us that the need we're attempting to get met is based on an inner child wound. In this case, the wound of feeling disregarded by a parent putting too many household tasks on our plate, making us feel unseen as a child. When we take a moment to get curious about what feels familiar about socks being left on the ground, we are tending to the activated inner child within us. This is actually the practice of reparenting ourselves while in relationship with another person. We speak up for the child in us that feels disrespected, unseen, and unloved—but we speak up as our inner adult, who doesn't feel that it's our partner's responsibility to pick up where our parents left off in doing the work of parenting us.

We've been taught to believe that relationships are all about compromise. I simply don't agree. I believe that thriving relationships are about two people being in alignment—with values, priorities, and what they believe an ideal partnership would look like for each of them. Compromise normally consists of one person denying an aspect of what is true for them in an attempt to make their partner comfortable—or what many would call making sure their partner's needs are getting met. Over time, this inevitably leads to bottled up resentment.

For example, let's say I'm in a relationship with a man who loves watching football all day on Sundays with his friends, but once we become a couple, I express that I would prefer that he spend that time with me. Maybe I get a lot of anxiety on Sundays, I don't like being alone all day, or I would just prefer to spend that quality time with my partner. Now, he can make the decision to compromise his authentic desire in an attempt to make me feel more comfortable. But is that decision really in service of either of us in the long run? He will more than likely be burying his irritation that he can no longer do something he enjoyed. I will miss an opportunity to cultivate tools for self-soothing the discomfort that comes up for me on Sundays. And we both miss an opportunity to come into alignment as a couple, with a creative way to spend time together on weekends—where neither one of us has to feel that we are being shortchanged.

Needs can be tricky to navigate, because as human animals, we do actually need one another. But so much of why we struggle to experience fulfillment in relationships is that we've been attempting to meet our human need for connection in ways that aren't sustainable. Hyperindependence, burying our frustrations, never speaking up in an attempt to maintain our attachments—none of these are sustainable strategies. But if we consistently look to someone else to do our healing work for us, we're normally reinforcing the experience of being wounded as soon as we feel that our needs aren't being met.

I once heard motivational speaker Iyanla Vanzant say, "I don't get to tell people how to love me. I get to see how they love, and then choose if I want to participate."[2] This concept is a radical departure from the position most couples therapy models would suggest we take. They tend to offer support around how to get our partners to love us in the way we desire to be loved. But ultimately, our ego minds tend to interpret this as an invitation to coerce another person into behaving a certain way so that we can feel more comfortable. And because what our Soul desires above everything else is the freedom to expand, controlling one another isn't a sustainable strategy.

Our work is to take ownership of what is within our control. I often like to ask myself, "If I had to take 100 percent responsibility for what is within my control right now, what could I own? How could I challenge myself to look at this situation differently? What is the story I'm telling myself that is causing me discomfort—and what else could possibly be true?" We can take responsibility for owning what's ours, and then communicating our desires to one another. Whether or not someone has the capacity to meet us in the space we desire is information; and then what we do with that information is what we have the ability to control.

Polarity

My understanding of the dance of polarity that exists in our relationships came to me as I sat with couples and started to notice a few key things about the energetic exchanges between them. I started to notice a draw toward polarity that occurs in almost all of our relationships—romantic, platonic, it doesn't seem to matter. We are drawn to people who experience the world in a way that cultivates a sense of polarity between us. One person likes sweet, while the other likes salty. The person who is always a little bit early, seems to be drawn to the person who's always hustling and running a tad bit behind. And in the context of energetics, one person seems to process the world through a more linear, structural, masculine lens—where planning ahead and knowing what to expect allows them to feel a sense of ease—while the other person processes the world through a more circular, open-ended, feminine lens—where going with the flow keeps them from feeling stifled and constrained.

This polarizing effect in our relationships (more than any other) has absolutely nothing to do with gender. We are drawn to those who complement us with the qualities that are more dormant within us—we are complemented by free-flowing energy if we tend to be more rigid, or with structural energy if we tend to be a bit more disorganized. But then we become perplexed and irritated in our relationships by our polarizing counterpart. We begin to get frustrated with the same contrasting traits we were initially attracted to. We start to be critical and indignant of their differences, feeling as though they should experience the world more like we do. This is when our work *could* be about bringing into our conscious recognition why we chose to bring this polarizing energy into our lives to begin with.

I've also noticed that there is a natural positioning that occurs in the way that our subconscious is consistently drawn to relationship patterns that recreate pain points from our childhood. We do this in our adult relationships in an attempt to create a different outcome on behalf of our inner child. Our subconscious believes, "If I can just get this person to see and understand me in the way that my original caretaker couldn't, *then* I will believe that I am worthy of the love I didn't feel from that caretaker." We've already explored all of the reasons that our life's work becomes about reclaiming and cultivating a sense of innate self-worth for ourselves. But doing that work will never keep us from experiencing the inevitable moments of activation that come up when we're attempting to be in relationship with others. It's easy to feel as though you've reached a state of enlightenment as you're sitting on a mountaintop by yourself, but in the words of Ram Dass, "If you think you're enlightened, go spend a week with your family."[3]

Playing with the dance of wounded masculine and feminine energetics brought to the surface in our romantic relationships is really just a tool for a form of shadow work. Shadow work is the Jungian term for uncovering the subconscious motivations that drive our behavior patterns. Our romantic partnerships are meant to bring up our ego's most challenging defense mechanisms because relationships are the space where we know we are most vulnerable to being harmed. They are the space where we stand in front of another person—whom we feel desperate to be unconditionally accepted by—and ask, *Can you love me?* The thought of them answering no to this question sends us straight back to the level of vulnerability we felt as a child, desperately needing the love of our caretakers.

As I began to watch couples interact while keeping Jung's description of masculine and feminine energetics in mind, I started to notice that the wounded energetic we inhabit in any given moment is in reaction to our partner creating a similar feeling to a parent or caretaker. This original caretaker elicited a polarizing dynamic within us from a wounded space. But it's important to keep in mind that these energies are not fixed, and most of us had challenging relationships with both of our parents in different ways. So based on the energy that our romantic relationship is presenting, our polarity will shift as a way of defending against the painful feelings we felt as a child. The way this continuation of childhood wounding is playing out in adult relationships looks something like this:

A challenging relationship with a parent who had a lot of Wounded Masculine Energy	This parental relationship created Wounded Feminine (anxious) Energy within me
• stuck in their mind • withholding of affection • always working $\longrightarrow$ • narcissistic tendencies • bullying	• often insecure • desperate for affection • struggle to find direction • over giving without boundaries • feeling like a victim
$\downarrow$	$\downarrow$
Creates strong physical attraction to people who exhibit these qualities $\longrightarrow$	Their behavior will activate these behaviors in me (my inner child's attempt to heal)

A challenging relationship with a parent who had a lot of Wounded Feminine Energy	This parental relationship cultivated within me the feeling of Wounded Masculine (avoidant) Energy
• critical • projects emotions onto others • seeks external safety $\longrightarrow$ • manipulative • irrational	• perfectionism • feels overwhelmed by emotions • withdraws from love • reactive • strong need to control
$\downarrow$	$\downarrow$
Creates strong attachment to people who exhibit these qualities $\longrightarrow$	Their behavior will activate these behaviors in me (my inner child's attempt to heal)

Again, none of these energetics are fixed. They are fluid and will shift in response to various relationship dynamics and challenges that come to the surface. The same was true for our caretakers.

In terms of doing our own shadow work, it can be helpful to notice when a behavior from a partner feels reminiscent of an energy we felt from one of our parents. That being said, we can't ever control another person, and normally our attempts to point out to someone that their "wounded energy" is reminding us of a parental figure we felt harmed by will only make them defensive. Ultimately, our work is to integrate our own inner masculine and feminine so that we can let go of the unconscious desire for someone else to fill this void for us. More on what that looks like later.

What we can take responsibility for in our relationships is shifting into a healthier space of polarity when we find ourselves being polarized into a wounded space. We will inevitably create polarizing energetics in our relationships, but we can decide whether we're going to create polarity from a wounded or a healthy space. We may not always stay there—but normally when we shift into a healthier space of polarity, our partner will move into the healthier polarizing energetic with us. Again, though, we can't control whether or not our partner has the capacity to meet us in that healthier space—we can only take responsibility for how we're showing up. Whether or not they're able to meet us in a healthier space is information.

To demonstrate the way this works, I'm going to bring back the quadrant we used in chapter 2. When we feel activated by our partner's behavior, our work is to determine which wounded quadrant we're currently operating from. From there, we attempt to meet our partner in the energy of the healthy quadrant that is the *diagonal energy* from the energy we're currently embodying. So if I realize that I'm meeting my partner in **wounded masculine energy** (controlling, wanting to withdraw, needing to be right) I am going to attempt to communicate from the space of **healthy feminine energy** (vulnerable communication, compassion, bringing in a bit of play). If, however, I find that I'm meeting my partner in a more **wounded feminine energy** (feeling insecure, afraid about the future, obsessing) I am going to focus on bringing myself into a more **healthy masculine energy** (using tools to create internal safety, integrity with my words, waiting to respond instead of react). In my healthy feminine energy, I am focused on receptivity, building trust, and connection. In my healthy masculine energy, I am focused on stability, self-containment, and clarity.

Healthy Masculine Energy

- creates safety
- witnesses without judgment
- holds space
- present without a goal
- integrity & awareness
- guides
- committed to truth
- listens deeply
- supportive & encouraging
- faces fears/knows death
- humble
- seeks mentorship
- reflective
- peaceful & grounded
- observes beyond what is seen
- responds instead of reacting

Healthy Feminine Energy

- intuitive
- loving
- playful & expressive
- fluid
- heart-centered
- surrenders
- connecting
- births, creates, manifests
- vulnerable
- compassionate
- sensual & affectionate
- connected to nature
- receives
- connected to Source energy
- authentic
- trusts

Wounded Masculine Energy

- aggressive
- stuck in mind/not present
- cold & distant
- competitive
- withdrawn
- bullying
- struggles to communicate needs
- has to be right
- reactive
- withdrawn—runs from love
- narcissistic
- needs to fix
- avoidant attachment
- afraid of failure
- ignores emotions

Wounded Feminine Energy

- irrational
- desperate
- needy
- manipulative
- insecure—seeks external validation
- inauthentic
- chases love/obsesses
- victim
- critical
- people pleasing
- projects emotions onto others
- lack of boundaries
- anxious attachment
- fears loss
- seeks external safety

We all have blind spots in terms of our own behavior, so if it feels difficult to determine which quadrant you're currently embodying, I find that it can be helpful to notice which quadrant you feel like your partner is currently in. But again, let me be clear. This inventory of your partner's energy is not so that you can attempt to shift them into the quadrant *you* feel like they need to move into. It's just that normally whatever wounded quadrant your partner is currently residing in, there's a pretty good chance you're inhabiting the polarized wounded quadrant. So if your partner is currently in the space of their wounded feminine energy (clinging, desperate, needy energy) the likelihood that this brings up wounded masculine energy within you (wanting to withdraw, feeling overwhelmed and resentful) is pretty good. In this case, your work is to make your way from wounded masculine energy up to the diagonal quadrant by taking up some healthy feminine space by being vulnerable about how your partner's behavior is making you feel (using feeling words, i.e. *overwhelmed, anxious, scared*).

I like to give a copy of the quadrants to the couples I work with for them to take home. When each person takes responsibility for owning which quadrant they're inhabiting, I never cease to be amazed at how they report a shift in how their partner begins to move into the opposing healthy quadrant. The most important aspect of how this energetic work functions is that you can only take responsibility for being wholeheartedly in your own quadrant. This is what I like to call the 100 percent you can own. You do this by moving yourself **for yourself**, and surrendering to the fact that if your partner never moves a single inch, that's *their* 100 percent to take or not. It's certainly information about your ability to find a sense of alignment with your partner, but the 100 percent responsibility each person takes for how they show up is theirs to own. This is how we shift out of the space of codependency (I can only feel okay if this person behaves the way I need them to) to a space of interdependence (I take responsibility for the person *I am* able to control, so that I can have the experience of authentic intimacy).

Jenna and Lewis were one of the first couples I supported in shifting their energetic dynamics using the masculine and feminine quadrants.

Both in their early thirties and having recently moved in together, Lewis and Jenna were falling into some of the most common behavior patterns that tend to drive a wedge between couples. Jenna was often overwhelmed with feelings of anxiety about where the relationship was headed. In the beginning, she described feeling like this was the best relationship she'd ever had. Lewis was attentive, clear with his intentions, and made her feel like she was the type of girl he longed to settle down and start a family with. As their relationship progressed, however, Jenna started to feel an insecurity that she recognized from all of her previous relationships. She would feel Lewis starting to pull away from her—seemingly annoyed by her attempts to connect, acting in ways that made her feel taken for granted, and refusing to take responsibility for the hurtful ways he was showing up in their dynamic.

For Lewis's part, he conceded that he often felt annoyed by Jenna's need for him. He pointed out that when they first met, she seemed independent and confident. She had her own activities and priorities, but now it seemed that most of her days were consumed with him—what he was doing, how he was feeling about her, who he was with, when they would be moving in together (and now when they would be getting married), and how he was treating her.

Lewis had the realization in one of our sessions that Jenna's behavior often reminded him of how his mother made him feel when he was young. His mother had lived in a constant fluctuation between anxiety and control—the wounded feminine energetic of desperately fearing that she would be left alone, and a wounded masculine energetic of narcissistic dominance over her children. But if he had to name the quadrant that he remembered his mother embodying most of the time, it was a wounded feminine, anxious energy. And similar to Jenna, he noted that this was not the first time he had attracted a woman with similar behavior patterns.

But Lewis wasn't the only one who found that their dynamic was bringing forward a sense of family of origin déjà vu. Jenna began to realize that all of the men she'd ever been with had similar tendencies to her own father when she took a hard look at the patterns. Her father fluctuated between what she described as a needy, childlike tendency to treat his wife (Jenna's mother) as an object—whose sole purpose was to cook, clean, and tend to his needs, while he took her being there for granted—and then shifting to an angry, withdrawn, bullying energy whenever anyone in his family dared question him or step outside of the rigid boundaries of what he deemed acceptable. If Jenna had to name the quadrant she remembered her father embodying most of the time, it was a wounded masculine, avoidant energy.

I would say that it was interesting that the two of them came into couples therapy complaining of their partner exhibiting very similar energetic tendencies to what they felt most wounded by in a challenging parental figure. Except I'm actually not surprised. As we've previously noted, these dynamics are what our psyche seeks out relationally in a subconscious attempt to heal. Let's take a closer look.

Pattern: Battling to Be the Alpha

What the majority of our relationships are pushing up against is societal conditioning that creates conflict with what our core energetics long to feel in a romantic partnership. For the purposes of this illustration (and to keep within the context of how Jenna and Lewis identify in terms of gender), I'm going to speak heteronormatively—using the descriptions of men/man when I'm speaking about those who identify with a core masculine energetic, and women/woman when I'm speaking about those who identify with a core feminine energetic. I want to make clear, however, that these same energetic conflicts occur with same-sex couples, in accordance to the core energetic with which they identify.

Society (and our ego minds) holds that the goal of our romantic relationships should be reaching a point of feeling secure enough with one another that we feel this person is essentially "ours." We've explored this—*my* partner, *my* husband, etc. This creates a psychological shift in our dynamics after the initial courting period, and once a certain amount of comfort with one another settles in. The trouble with having too much security in a relationship is that not only does it eventually lead to a lack of presence and personal responsibility, it creates a deadening of the energetic polarity that two people long to feel from one another.

When Lewis acts from the belief that once he has "ownership" of a woman, his developmental work and mission is complete—that he no longer needs to work to win her over, can look to her for his direction, or he loses sight of his larger life mission outside of the relationship—he is not embodying a healthy masculine core.

A great deal of the behavior patterns that society has encouraged men to embody in their romantic relationships are **actually characteristics of wounded feminine energy**. These include:

- seeking constant external validation through new conquests
- using sex, performance, and completion as a means to validate their adequacy
- looking to a relationship with another person to provide a sense of identity, direction, and containment for their lack of discipline
- the inability to self-soothe
- attempts to cultivate self-worth through how they are viewed by others
- a lack of emotional boundaries and clarity around a sense of Self
- a consistent existential anxiety that comes from being disconnected to their Soul

And it's not that men don't have or shouldn't be in touch with elements of their feminine—of course they do and need to—but if a man embodies too much wounded feminine energy in a relationship with a woman, she will feel unsafe in his lack of containment.

In response to this lack of containment, much of what society has conditioned women like Jenna to do is to take over and begin to bridge the gap for their partner with characteristics of **wounded masculine energy**:

- being stuck in the mind, unable to stay present with what's happening
- feeling the need to control or create relational clarity by coming up with a plan
- taking responsibility for keeping their partner on track, containing his unruly energy or "mothering" him
- ignoring the truth of their own emotions, putting forward a stoic/"cool girl" persona
- displaying reactive, irritated, bullying energy and viewing the masculine with contempt
- exhibiting a fundamental lack of trust and respect for the man they are with

As a woman senses a man's lack of clarity and intention, she will feel an instinctual urge to create relational safety or take control. A woman can love a man, but if she does not have a fundamental level of respect for him, if she doesn't trust in his sense of leadership, she will view him as a child. And so she will begin to treat him like a little boy that can't be depended upon. She has now made the shift from the healthy feminine energetic she was embodying when they first met to a wounded masculine energetic.

When we condition men to believe that their role in romantic relationships is to embody a wounded feminine energetic, there is no space for a woman to feel safe in her feminine essence with him. He is essentially taking up all of the feminine space in the room. As she starts to take over the polarizing energy in their relationship from a wounded masculine space, this brings up an archaic resistance within him. It's almost as though he senses her attempting to emasculate him, and he cannot stand for it. He begins to overpower *her* wounded masculine energy with *his own*, similar to the way you sometimes see an animal shrinking down when the more dominant animal asserts themselves and demands submission. The woman begins to shift into a wounded feminine energetic—terrified of being abandoned by him and desperate to find a way to make him stay. As soon as a man senses the shift into a wounded feminine energetic from a woman (she's not going anywhere so he can relax) he begins to settle back into his societally conditioned wounded feminine energy again—taking her for granted and reigniting her wounded masculine rage.

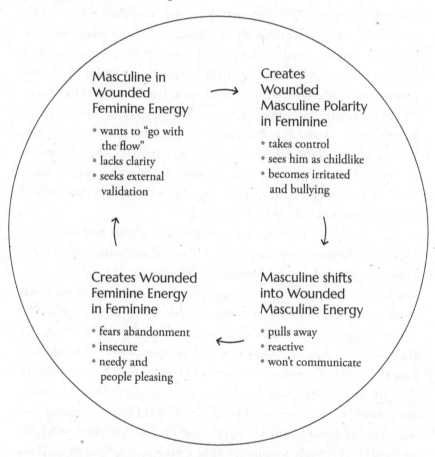

Masculine in Wounded Feminine Energy
• wants to "go with the flow"
• lacks clarity
• seeks external validation

Creates Wounded Masculine Polarity in Feminine
• takes control
• sees him as childlike
• becomes irritated and bullying

Creates Wounded Feminine Energy in Feminine
• fears abandonment
• insecure
• needy and people pleasing

Masculine shifts into Wounded Masculine Energy
• pulls away
• reactive
• won't communicate

This becomes a cycle. Society encourages a lack of healthy masculine responsibility in men, and an abundance of caretaking in women. Core masculine men and core feminine women attempt to play out these roles in their relationships, not understanding why something feels off to them. They resist the distortion of polarity by cultivating a wounded energetic between them, and in doing this, they recreate the energetic in their partner that they felt most harmed by in their childhood. Essentially, they cultivate a return to a wounded sense of homeostasis.

The reason this wounded cycle always begins with the masculine embodiment of feminine energy is that this cycle of distortion came into our relationships when men were conditioned to believe they no longer held a responsibility to protect the feminine. And this goes back to our societies' initial decision to disregard and dominate feminine energy. Men who feared the potency of feminine intuition (those with an independent spirit, their capacity to create life, and heal through their connection to Mother Earth) called them witches, imprinted a visceral fear of masculine harm upon them, and left the feminine with a core abandonment wound that has carried on generationally. In doing this, the masculine collective disconnected from their Soul space—essentially disengaging them from the healthy feminine energetic within themselves and creating a sense of inner confusion about who they are and what they are meant to do with their lives.

Lewis was subconsciously acting out a sense of rage he'd been carrying toward the feminine—both on an individual and collective level. His personal rage was toward the mother he felt abandoned by when she was unable to take responsibility for healing her own energy so that she could nurture, care for, and see him in the way that he longed to be seen. His collective rage was toward the society that had taught him to disconnect from his inner feminine. To "man up," conquer women, and distract himself instead of learning to stay with and understand his own pain. In his relationship with Jenna, Lewis attempted to create a dynamic where the woman he is with reminds him of the wounded feminine energy that feels familiar to him—the energetic most frequently embodied by his mother. He is actually attempting to heal his relationship with the feminine on a subconscious level—but he can only do this when the focus shifts away from Jenna and back to what their dynamic is demonstrating to him about himself.

Jenna has done the same thing in her relationship with Lewis—she's landed on a relational dynamic with her partner that reminds her of her father.

She has chosen a man that reinforces her subconscious belief that men cannot be trusted. As Lewis abandoned her and forced her to take the lead in their relationship, she felt an inner rage on behalf of generations of women who were abandoned by a society of men that abandoned their role as warrior and protector, and left the feminine for dead. Women have been attempting to love men while carrying a generational wound of mistrust on behalf of the feminine that our society has failed to reconcile. This has resulted in the wounded cycle our relationships create over and over—we rinse and repeat as we fall back into patterns of behaving the way society and our family of origins have taught us to behave toward one another. It leads to a terribly frustrating and unfulfilling relational experience for all parties. But there's another option.

Solution: Cultivating Healthy Polarity

The solution to this generational pain point is for each person to take responsibility for creating a healthy sense of polarity within themselves. We cannot come into right relationship with others until we first address the origin point of what the relational dynamic between us is activating internally. A codependent paradigm has taught us that we require another person to cooperate with the changes we believe they need to make before we can heal our relationships. An interdependent approach is based on the premise that as we take responsibility for understanding what the relationship dynamic is bringing up for ourselves, we are able to meet the other person in a more conscious way. This inevitably creates a form of pattern interruption, shifting the energetic dynamics between the two people. When we find ourselves acting from a wounded masculine space within our relational polarity, our work is to attempt to connect to the other person from a healthy feminine space. When we are in a wounded feminine space, our work becomes to bring the focus back inward and create a grounded sense of containment within ourselves.

When Lewis and Jenna came in to see me, they were deep in the cyclical pattern of battling over who would be the alpha. Both felt unsafe to be an authentic version of themselves with the other, because frankly, they had both lost track of who they were individually in the midst of this relationship. Since their origin point of relational wounding—or what felt closest to home for each of them—was Lewis in wounded masculine energy and Jenna in wounded feminine energy, we worked to figure out how each of them could take personal responsibility for the energy they were bringing to the dynamic.

When Lewis found himself in wounded masculine energy (finding Jenna's emotions overwhelming, feeling a sense of contempt or irritation, or wanting to withdraw from the relationship altogether), his work was to make his way toward the healthy feminine quadrant. Tangibly, this meant that he would be vulnerable with Jenna about the moments when he felt overwhelmed and explain what felt reminiscent for him of his own childhood. He would take up time and space in his own life with self-care rituals like moving his body and remembering how it felt to play when he was young. He would attempt to reach for Jenna and connect in moments that he felt himself instinctually want to pull away. And he would practice trusting that no part of him was ever diminished by being vulnerable—regardless of the relational outcome between the two of them.

For her part, when Jenna found herself flooded with the anxious wounded feminine energy that came to the surface whenever she feared Lewis's abandonment, she would practice grounding herself in her own healthy masculine energy. This meant that she would practice witnessing her emotions without judging them. She would unapologetically speak from a place of integrity to face her fear of being too much for Lewis if she were to tell him the truth. She would act as her own fierce protector by holding boundaries around the way she allowed herself to be spoken to. And she would cultivate a toolkit to soothe herself when she felt overwhelmed by fears of abandonment.

The healthy polarity they each cultivated by taking 100 percent responsibility for their own energy allowed the other person to see them clearly, instead of seeing them through the projection of their own wounds. A codependent cultivation of polarity is one where we attempt to force our partner into the polarizing energy we believe we are missing within ourselves. But this is also the polarity that reminds us of an original wound.

Interdependent cultivation of polarity suggests that as we practice integrating our own healthy masculine *and* feminine energy, we are able to co-create our relationship with the actual person in front of us—instead of who we believe we need them to be for us to feel complete.

Soul Contracts

No person is sent to us by accident. This is the shift in perception that completely transforms our relationship to the practice of loving another person. We move from the practice of attempting to get our own needs met to seeing each person we come in contact with as a Divine assignment. I say the word *practice* quite intentionally, because we all have an ego mind that will cause us to forget the larger purpose of our Soul mission, even when we come into the space of conscious recognition. We will feel tired and afraid, shortchanged and unseen, insecure and wanting to grasp—but our work becomes to recognize when we fall into the inevitable traps of our ego mind and find our way back to the practice of authentic love. And so, what is this conscious recognition? What does it mean to truly love one another from the space of recognition that we are Souls?

We have been taught to believe that when you fall in love with someone, what happens is that this person loves you in a way that you've always longed to be loved. They discover you, are captivated by your effervescence, can't get enough of all that you are—so much so, that they want to spend the rest of their lives loving you in this way and making you feel their love. The reason this flawed premise of loving is destined to fall short is that it starts with a fundamental misunderstanding of the truth of who we are.

You longing to be loved by another person in order to experience love is kind of like the ocean longing to experience water. You are Source energy in human form. That means that you are the essence of love embodied. You cannot experience authentic love with another person based on a flawed premise of loving. The truth of what it is to love someone is that you are focusing your energy on loving them. You are bringing yourself into alignment with the highest version of you, so that you can show up in the most loving way possible.

And here's what's really important to understand: being in alignment with the highest version of who we are is never loving based on what we are afraid of. People pleasing, controlling, manipulation, score keeping, coercion—all of these codependent tendencies are driven from the space of fearing that we are not enough on our own. The practice of defending against what we're afraid of will never lead to the experience of authentic love. If you believe that you need someone else to fill you up with something you are lacking, that is not based on your love for them—that is based on your desire to use them as a means to an end. The difficult truth is that what we've been taught to understand about love is really a subtle form of manipulation based on the wounds of our ego. It is love rooted in a foundation of defending against the fear that we are not enough—and that is the opposite of love.

There is a powerful phrase I've heard frequently referenced in Jungian psychology that says the meeting of two personalities is like the contact of two chemical substances: if there is any reaction, both are transformed. When we shift our perception of life into one where we see ourselves as attending a life school designed with the intention of the evolution of our Souls, we start to see our relationships through a completely different lens. Each person we come in contact with becomes a part of our Soul's curriculum—challenging us, inspiring us, and mirroring back to us where we have room to grow. Our work is not to go out in search of the perfect partner who encapsulates everything we think we need to experience a fulfilling partnership—the truth is, most of the time we have no idea what we need. What we think we need is usually based on the level of consciousness we are holding in any given moment, which is informed by what we are being called to heal.

The perfect person for us is always the romantic partner, friend, parent, or acquaintance we are in relationship to in this moment. They are perfect because they are the Divine assignment our Soul has orchestrated for us to learn from right now. All of our relationships, even—and I would argue especially—the most challenging ones, have come into our lives to teach us how to bring ourselves back into alignment with love. And sometimes the loving response is a boundary. Sometimes the loving relationship is one where we are no longer in communication. Sometimes the most loving decision for all parties involved is for us to focus on our own healing and release the other person gracefully, so that they have the opportunity to heal themselves. Because you are not actually loving another person when you allow them to practice living in a vibration that is out of alignment with love—in a relationship with you. Sometimes the Soul curriculum we are meant to take away from our interaction with a particular person is learning how to lovingly walk away.

The point of understanding that each relationship is a sacred contract designed in service of our Soul's evolution is knowing that no interaction or time spent with another person is ever in vain. In her book *A Return to Love*, Marianne Williamson points out, "Relationships are assignments. They are part of a vast plan for our enlightenment, the Holy Spirit's blueprint by which each individual Soul is led to greater awareness and expanded love. Relationships are the Holy Spirit's laboratories in which people are brought together who have the maximal opportunity for mutual growth."[4]

Whether we spend a week or a lifetime interacting with another person, we are inevitably changed by knowing them when we ask ourselves the question, "What did this person come into my life to teach me?" When we attempt to grasp onto relationships beyond the expiration date stipulated in our Soul contracts, we have entered the space of resistance. We can tell we are in resistance because it is always based on what we're afraid of. This is the equivalent of swimming against the current. We can do this for as long as we choose to or need to, but it will always lead to a greater sense of stress and fatigue. When we trust that people flow in and out of our lives in accordance with Divine timing and each Soul's alignment, this is the equivalent of allowing the current to carry us where we are meant to be—bringing our lives back into a state of flow.

Safety and Aliveness

So we're back. We've come full circle to exploring the duality that often makes our relationships such a challenge. What I have come to understand about the conundrum we've faced with balancing our need for attachment (relational stability, structures we can depend on, and emotional safety) and our need for authenticity (space for continuously evolving, the freedom to be who we are, and a sense of aliveness) is that what we've ultimately been attempting to reconcile is balancing our own masculine and feminine energetics, while staying in right relationship to another person. This challenge feels a bit easier to navigate once we realize that it isn't actually a problem we'll ever solve. It's the relational equivalent of what it means to be a Soul in a human body for a period of time.

The masculine aspects of ourselves are the parts of us that are rooted in this physical world. We each came into these bodies with a dharma, or mission, to be carried out within our lifetime. Our dharma can be as simple as seeking to find a sense of peace around what it is we are doing here, or as complex as attempting to create solutions for the most taxing issues we are currently facing as a human race. The most important aspect of what we choose to follow in the pursuit of our life's dharma is finding a way to be of service.

I mentioned this phrase once already back in chapter 6, but I'm consistently reminded of the words of Dr. Wayne Dyer when I think about cultivating a greater sense of purpose for our lives: The mantra of the lower self is, "I need more." The mantra of the higher Self is, "How do I serve?" The energetic of **needing more** is the **wounded feminine energetic** that causes us to be in a constant state of existential anxiety. Shifting our life's focus to a healthy masculine energetic of service brings a sense of clarity, a containment of our nervous energy, the conscious practice of humility, and a reckoning with the inevitable deterioration of these human bodies. This causes us to be more intentional with our time. Allowing our lives to be focused on carrying out a mission rooted in service supports us in moving into the space of inspired action, because our dharma becomes bigger than the fears of our ego mind. It becomes rooted in protecting something greater than ourselves. This is healthy masculine leadership.

The feminine aspects of who we are, however, are the parts of us that trust in the unfolding of larger spiritual truths. This is the part of us that intuitively knows about sacred rhythms, supportive entities, an inner guidance system, and the synchronistic way that our lives are unfolding. This is the part of us that trusts that we are held by life, instead of the **wounded masculine paradigm** that believes that **life is something we need to defend against**. The most powerful question we can continuously ask ourselves in an attempt to reclaim our feminine essence is, "But am I having fun? Am I allowing myself to truly enjoy the sacred time that I've been given?" As you ask yourself this question, it will instinctually feel like it's a ridiculous question to ask. It will feel reckless and immature. It will feel like it disregards our responsibilities, discounts the world's suffering, and is the prescription for fundamentally wasting our time. It feels this way because we have been indoctrinated with a wounded masculine perspective that teaches us that our lives are something we are meant to suffer through, instead of something we came here to enjoy.

The trouble with this wounded masculine logic is that we cannot suffer enough to eliminate the world's suffering. We can never carry enough responsibility to make ourselves feel worthy of rest, inspiration, and joy, if that's not the innate truth of what we believe we deserve. The creation of a world that our highest Selves would dream of inhabiting cannot be cultivated from the space of fear, lack, or an endless state of productivity for productivity's sake. It requires a return to the imaginal space of our feminine creativity. A willingness to put down our armored guards and connect with people who have different political affiliations from the ones we hold. It asks us to be vulnerable with the shame we've been hiding away, and trust that as we unearth our shame, we give those around us permission to surrender their own burdens. The world we are being called to create is asking us to return to our hearts. To replace the question "What am I going to get out of this?" with "How can I be more loving in this moment?" This is healthy feminine leadership.

The integration of our inner masculine and feminine requires that each of us take responsibility for showing up fully as the type of person we want to be. This requires a tremendous amount of courage, but it's the only way this work gets done. And because we are energetic beings who are all connected, what we do for ourselves, we do in service of the greater collective. My healing creates a ripple that inspires every other Soul I come in contact with to heal themselves. This is how we create a world that is not only more safe for our children and our children's children, but how we ensure that the dreams that we hold for the future continue to evolve.

Sovereignty

Because the therapy room is a microcosm of the outside world, how we show up relationally with our therapist tends to give us insight into how we negotiate all of the other relationships in our lives. I have come to believe that this is true of the ways our romantic relationships mirror back to us what is happening on a collective level. We are living through a unique moment in the evolution of the human race. The societal structures as we've known them have become unsustainable in a way we can no longer ignore. More than any other time in history, the choice before us as a human race has become a clear one—evolve or die. This is also true of the way we are meeting one another relationally. If we're going to see the value in joining together in partnership, our relationships will be forced to evolve.

More and more frequently, single people are noting that they don't see a reason to surrender the freedom they find in singlehood. This choice feels understandable, when you look at the current distortions of love that exist within the relation landscape. Casual hookups seem to carry less of a social taboo, women are more capable than ever of taking care of themselves, and our relationships with technology have in many ways offered a subterfuge for the intimacy we once found in the presence of other people. So the question becomes: why should we prioritize healing our intimate relationships? What is the benefit to us as individuals in doing the work required to evolve and take responsibility for attempting to cultivate a more conscious way of partnering?

There are a few very clear answers to this question. First, our survival depends upon it. We cannot continue to live within a wounded masculine paradigm that suggests that division, destruction, and deprivation of the earth we are inhabiting is a sustainable way to live. Second, because almost all of us have been wounded within the space of relationships, relationships hold the secret sauce that is required for us to heal. They hold up a potent mirror and offer data in the form of our activation points about the truth of how we're feeling inside. And finally, love is one of the most transcendent, clarifying, life-affirming experiences we can possibly have while we are alive. As the character Jean Valjean sings in the musical *Les Misérables*, "To love another person is to see the face of God." When we dare to believe that relational magic is still possible for us to experience, it creates a ripple effect that raises the vibration of everyone around us.

Committing ourselves to an authentic version of loving means keeping our hearts open to a love that coincides with various forms of evolution. I have learned more about the healing power of love through my relationship with my child's father, and the grace-filled way that each of us decided to set the other free, than I could have possibly learned if we stayed in the marital container that each of us knew we'd outgrown. Allowing our love to change form illustrated for me of the type of relationships it's possible to create when we make the decision to choose love over fear. When we decide to choose the path that supports our continued evolution over the path that makes us feel most comfortable or safe. This is the introduction of a feminine principle in the way we choose to love. It prioritizes collaboration and trust, values transparency and authentic aliveness, and continues to believe that anything is possible when we prioritize loving from the space of our Soul.

But a patriarchal model of partnership is not interested in the process of our Soul's evolution. It has no interest in us taking responsibility for our lives and believing that we were always meant to be free. Because free people push back on the systems that are oppressing them and using fear to keep them under control. Free people define their lives for themselves and surrender the need to have the approval of an external authority. Free people heal. They return to seeing themselves through the lens of wholeness, instead of filling their days with addictions and distractions to make up for a lack of aliveness.

It can be difficult to conceptualize a vision for what a sovereign sense of loving can be, when it's a paradigm we are meant to design for ourselves. To be sovereign means to be governed by an inner authority. This is the equivalent of defining our Souls' truth for ourselves. The integration of a feminine perspective within our partnerships means living in alignment with our Souls' highest potential. Seeing a side-by-side comparison of loving from the space of our patriarchal programming vs. the space of sovereignty can offer something for us to wrap our heads around:

Patriarchal Partnerships vs. Sovereign Love

<ul><li>society created guidelines</li><li>rooted in obligation</li><li>strives to control</li><li>works to find a compromise</li><li>purpose is companionship</li><li>roles are dictated by gender norms</li><li>perpetuates attachment wounds</li><li>codependent and incomplete</li></ul>

Patriarchal Partnerships	Sovereign Love
• society created guidelines • rooted in obligation • strives to control • works to find a compromise • purpose is companionship • roles are dictated by gender norms • perpetuates attachment wounds • codependent and incomplete	• co-created by those in partnership • for the purpose of transformation • practices trust • works to find alignment • purpose is shared vision • roles are supportive of ease and flow • supports authentic healing • interdependent and sovereign

From the perspective of our Soul, the purpose of an aligned partnership will never be to diminish our personal power. A Soul-driven love inspires us to become more of who and what we are capable of being, not less.

The structural systems that suggested there was only one way for our lives to be lived are in the midst of their final days. An interdependent model of loving is one where we look to an inner authority for insight into what feels like the truths we choose to put our faith in. The point of unpacking how we've been socialized to hold gender roles, where we carry unconscious generational pain, and why we feel a fundamental lack of fulfillment in our relationships, is to understand that the wounded masculine paradigm we've been existing in has never been in alignment with the truth of who we are. The rise of a feminine perspective does not mean trading in a patriarchal system of dominance for a matriarchal one. No, the rise of the feminine is the reclaiming of the feminine aspects that exist within all of us so that we can embody a felt sense of balance and integration. On a tangible level, this integration of our masculine and feminine energetics looks like freedom.

The creation of a New Earth paradigm requires that we value freedom in every facet of our lives—in our structural systems, on our career paths, in our educational systems, and most certainly in our relationships—putting less of an emphasis on a false sense of certainty and finding more value in asking the question, "Does whatever I'm doing make me feel free?" The freedom each of our Souls are essentially seeking is to decide what living an intentional life looks like for ourselves. This is the conscious transfer of trust from an externalized source of power to a source of power within. It is the knowing that my answers live within, my power lives within, my Trust resides within.

The wounded masculine and wounded feminine practices of externalizing power are unsustainable social models. A wounded masculine paradigm places value on striving for certainty and an ability to assert control. This requires that we sever ourselves from our hearts, because we cannot keep our heart space open to empathize with someone while simultaneously attempting to dominate and control them. A wounded feminine paradigm of looking externally for someone to save us from internal chaos and fear isn't sustainable either. If we require someone outside of ourselves to feel a solid sense of self, our sense of self has no solid footing. Our soul will not conspire with our ego in the externalization of our power. It will eventually remove anything outside of us that we place our worth in, to remind us that our worth doesn't belong there.

A healthy paradigm of masculine and feminine energy is rooted in the trust that resides within. A healthy masculine paradigm is the energetic of taking responsibility for our lives. Understanding that while no one is coming to save us, we have always had everything we need to create a sense of clarity and meaning for ourselves. This is the energetic shift from a wounded feminine energetic of "I need someone outside of myself to put my trust in," to a healthy masculine energetic of "I trust myself." A healthy feminine paradigm is the energetic of trusting and surrendering to life itself. Allowing our intuition, potential to create, and belief in the synchronistic order of life's unfolding to be the guiding force in our lives. This is the energetic shift from a wounded masculine energetic of "I can only feel safe when I am in control," to a healthy feminine energetic of "I trust my Soul." Here's an illustration of this energetic quadrant:

(taking responsibility for my own life)	(trusting and surrendering to life)
Healthy Masculine Energy meaning & clarity I Trust Myself	Healthy Feminine Energy trust & receptivity I Trust My Soul
Wounded Masculine Energy certainty & control	Wounded Feminine Energy chaos & fear

The most common misconception about an interdependent model of love and partnerships (which is essentially the integration of our own masculine and feminine energy) is that this way of loving is selfish. Our ego mind attempts to convince us that if we bring the focus inward and take responsibility for controlling what is within our control, we will somehow be leaving others behind. But the truth is, the liberation that we find in this sovereign way of loving releases us from the fear that keeps us from loving one another well. Love that desperately grasps onto another or attempts to control them is "loving" based on what we're afraid will happen if we don't. As we liberate ourselves from the illusion that we are anything less than perfect, whole, and complete in this moment exactly as we are, we're able to show up in the space of presence and offer love to another.

We were always meant to come into remembrance of the vast lumi-nescent beings that we are. We were always meant to be sovereign, even as we co-create our lives with others. We were always meant to reclaim our ability to dance and feel and express and trust and serve and bear witness and receive and expand and LOVE. We were always meant to remember our capacity to love ourselves and one another with every bit of our whole hearts. This is our time of remembrance. This is the rise of the feminine principle. This is the return to our Souls. This is how we remember. This is how we love. And so it is.

I love you without knowing
how, or when, or from where.
I love you simply, without
problems or pride: I love
you in this way because
I do not know any other way
of loving but this. in which
there is no I or you, so
intimate that your hand
upon my chest is my hand.
so intimate that when I
fall asleep your eyes close.

PABLO NERUDA[5]

Acknowledgments

to Mykee. Thank you for teaching me about the immense capacity we hold as people to continue showing up for one another in and as love. You have been a protective force in my life that has offered an unwavering sense of support and consistency beyond what I can ever truly express. Thank you for the presence, tenderness, and devotion you bring to loving our child. So much of the woman I've become has been because of the man that you are.

To my mom and dad. Thank you for teaching me about strength and fortitude. Thank you for loving me so fiercely and exposing me to so many opportunities that afforded me the insight, security, and discernment to thrive. And thank you for being my first example of a love that weathered seasons, adversity, and limiting beliefs, in a way that allowed me to write my own rules.

To Ronni. Thank you for bearing witness to the various life phases I've processed with you in the most compassionate, wise, and Soul-enriching container. Thank you for advocating for the little girl inside of me and giving her permission to play without limitations and be her own fierce protector.

To my teacher and mentor, Esther Perel. Thank you for expanding my perception of what it is possible for a woman, a mother, and a leader in the world to be. Thank you for seeing me, asking me questions that challenged me to create my own perspectives, and believing in my potential when I did not yet believe in myself. Your endless curiosity, voracious intellect, and commitment to aliveness has been a profound example and source of inspiration for me to draw from.

To John Kim and Hilary Swanson. Thank you for making me believe this was possible. Hilary, thank you for supporting me in crafting the vision of a book that could be supportive of others. John, thank you for your willingness to color outside the lines, build the bus while driving it, and share your story so courageously—giving me permission to be seen, and an understanding of why it matters.

To the most phenomenal literary agent in the business, JL Stermer. Thank you for energetically saying to me "I got you" through every single step of this process. Thank you for getting it, being my champion, and for every single thing you've done to make my dream come true. You will hold a sacred space in my heart forever.

To Diana Ventimiglia (along with the incredible team at Sounds True). Thank you for believing in this book. Thank you for your vision, and for knowing that we are ready for this conversation and for deeper layers of collective healing. Thank you for allowing me to be myself in the process of writing and for everything you've done to make this book the physical embodiment of what I could feel it was destined to be.

To the sisterhood of women who've held me down, inspired me with your intuitive gifts, and helped me understand, acknowledge, and whole-heartedly embrace the perfection of this path during the times when I needed you most. I am blessed to say that there are far too many of you to name—but I'll start with Stephanie, Milly, Emily, Ashley, Susheela, and my ultimate ride or die, Vanessa. Thank you all for your particular brand of magic.

And to Cairo. Thank you for being my reason. Thank you for choosing me. Thank you for making me want to be a better version of myself every single day. You changed everything and you helped me find my way back to me.

Notes

Opening Epigraph: Maya Angelou, "Dr. Maya Angelou on Loving and Letting Go," Oprah.com, October 11, 2015, video, 2:15, oprah.com /own-master-class/dr-maya-angelou-on-loving-and-letting-go-video.

Introduction

Epigraph: McKenzie Jean-Phillippe and Cailey Griffin, "30 Oprah Quotes That Have All the Wisdom You'll Ever Need," Oprah Daily, July 27, 2022, oprahdaily.com/life/g23429862/oprah-quotes/?slide=13.

1 John Kim, *Single on Purpose: Redefine Everything. Find Yourself First* (New York: HarperOne, 2021), 77.

Chapter 1: The Goal Is to Be Chosen

Epigraph: Joseph Campbell, *The Hero's Journey: Joseph Campbell on His Life and Work* (New York: Harper & Row, 1990).

1 Gabor Maté, "Gabor Maté—Authenticity vs. Attachment," Phil Borges, May 14, 2019, YouTube video, 4:18, youtube.com/watch?v= l3bynimi8HQ.

2 bell hooks, *The Will to Change: Men, Masculinity, and Love* (New York: Washington Square Press, 2004), 23.

Chapter 2: Nobody Forgets the Truth of Who They Are, They Just Get Better at Lying to Themselves

Epigraph: Nikita Gill, *Wild Embers: Poems of Rebellion, Fire, and Beauty* (New York: Hachette Books, 2017).

1 C. G. Jung, *The Collected Works of C. G. Jung*, vol. 9, part 2, *Aion*, ed. and trans. Gerhard Adler and R. F. C. Hull, 2nd ed. (Princeton, NJ: Princeton University Press, 1979), para. 126.

2   Esther Perel, *Mating in Captivity: Unlocking Erotic Intelligence* (New York: Harper, 2006).

3   Llewellyn Vaughan-Lee, *The Return of the Feminine and the World Soul* (Point Reyes, CA: The Golden Sufi Center, 2009), 3.

Chapter 3: Scenes from a Relationship

Epigraph: James Hillman, *The Soul's Code: In Search of Character and Calling* (New York: Random House, 1996).

1   Justin Wm. Moyer, "Study: Up to 60 Percent of Women Fantasize about 'Being Dominated,'" Washington Post, November 3, 2014, washingtonpost.com/news/morning-mix/wp/2014/11/03/study-up-to-60-percent-of-women-fantasize-about-being-dominated/.

2   Erick Bauer, "'Fifty Shades of Grey' Was the Best-Selling Book of the Decade in the U.S., The NPD Group Says," The NPD Group, December 18, 2019, npd.com/news/press-releases/2019/fifty-shades-of-grey-was-the-best-selling-book-of-the-decade-in-the-u-s-the-npd-group-says/.

3   Joseph Campbell, *The Hero's Journey: Joseph Campbell on His Life and Work* (New York: Harper & Row, 1990).

4   Wayne Dyer, "EGO is Edging God Out | Wayne Dyer," Morning Compass, December 15, 2022, YouTube video, 4:45, youtube.com/watch?v=rsJJSS4k6D8.

Chapter 4: Vigorous Honesty

Epigraph: Anaïs Nin, *Winter of Artifice* (Troy, MI: Sky Blue Press, 2007).

1   Monica Froese, "Maternity Leave in the United States: Facts You Need to Know," Healthline, July 4, 2023, healthline.com/health/pregnancy/united-states-maternity-leave-facts.

2   Esther Perel, "Esther Perel: The Quality of Your Relationships Determines the Quality of Your Life," Summit, February 12, 2019, YouTube video, 0:36, youtube.com/watch?v=LmDPAOE5V2Y.

3   Abraham Hicks, "Abraham Hicks—When You Meet Him, You Will Have This Knowing You Are the One (Relationships)," Abraham

attracting love, January 11, 2021, YouTube video, 13:07, youtube
.com/watch?v=ZnZNBIGpLlo.

4 Peter Crone, "Use This Example to Reveal Where You Are Not
Free | Peter Crone & Aubrey Marcus," Aubrey Marcus Clips,
August 5, 2021, YouTube video, 4:03, youtube.com/watch?v=
hkHGRDZvt5A.

Chapter 5: Maybe We're Better Off Alone?

Epigraph: According to Quote Investigator, Pablo Picasso made
this statement to the Spanish newspaper *ABC* in 1932. "Nothing
Can Be Accomplished Without Solitude," Quote Investigator,
December 16, 2015, quoteinvestigator.com/2015/12/16/solitude/.

1 *The Matrix*, directed by Lana Wachowski and Lilly Wachowski
(Burbank, CA: Warner Bros, 1999), 2 hours, 16 minutes.

2 Robert Hinojosa, "Men's Mental Health: An Overview," Choosing
Therapy, November 2, 2021, choosingtherapy.com/mens-mental
-health/; Joy Moses and Jackie Janosko, "Demographic Data Project:
Part II: Gender and Individual Homelessness," Homelessness
Research Institute, September, 2019, endhomelessness.org/wp
-content/uploads/2019/09/DDP-Gender-brief-09272019-byline
-single-pages.pdf; Leah Wang, Wendy Sawyer, Tiana Herring, and
Emily Widra, "Beyond the Count: A Deep Dive into State Prison
Populations," Prison Policy Initiative, April 2022, prisonpolicy.org
/reports/beyondthecount.html.

3 Terrence Real, *I Don't Want to Talk About It: Overcoming the Secret
Legacy of Male Depression* (New York: Scribner, 1997).

4 Henry David Thoreau, *Walden* (New York: Thomas Y. Crowell &
Company, 1910).

5 Trevor Noah, *Born a Crime: Stories from a South African Childhood*
(New York: Spiegel & Grau, 2016).

6 C.G. Jung, *Memories, Dreams, Reflections*, ed. Aniela Jaffé, trans.
Richard Winston and Clara Winston (New York: Vintage, 1989).

Chapter 6: A Toolkit to Bring You Back Home

Epigraph: *Before Sunrise*, directed by Richard Linklater (Culver City, CA: Columbia Pictures, 1995), 1 hour, 41 minutes.

1 Bessel Van der Kolk, *The Body Keeps the Score: Brain, Mind, and Body in the Healing of Trauma* (New York: Penguin Books, 2015).

2 Laura McKowen, *We Are the Luckiest: The Surprising Magic of a Sober Life* (Novato, CA: New World Library, 2020).

3 Søren Kierkegaard, *Søren Kierkegaards Skrifter (Journalen JJ, 167)*, vol. 18 (1843; Copenhagen, Denmark: Søren Kierkegaard Research Center, 1997), 306.

4 Foundation for Inner Peace, *A Course in Miracles*, (Mill Valley, CA: the Foundation for Inner Peace, 2007).

Chapter 7: The Dance of Eros

Epigraph: Jack Kornfield, "Love vs Attachment," personal website, November 30, 2018, jackkornfield.com/love-vs-attachment/.

Chapter 8: Reclaiming the Masculine

Epigraph: bell hooks, *The Will to Change: Men, Masculinity, and Love* (New York: Washington Square Press, 2004).

1 hooks, *The Will to Change*, 26.

2 Viktor E. Frankl, *Man's Search for Meaning* (Boston, MA: Beacon Press, 1959).

Chapter 9: Reclaiming the Feminine

Epigraph: Marion Woodman, *The Pregnant Virgin: A Process of Psychological Transformation* (Toronto, Canada: Inner City Books 1985), ch.7.

1 Alice Walker, *The Temple of My Familiar* (San Diego, CA: Harcourt Brace Jovanovich, 1989).

2 C.G. Jung, "Letter to Bill Wilson from Dr. Carl Jung," January 30, 1961, via Carl Jung Depth Psychology (website), March 29, 2020, carljungdepthpsychologysite.blog/2020/03/29/carl-jung-his-craving -for-alcohol-was-the-equivalent-on-a-low-level-of-the-spiritual-thirst/.

3   Parabola Editors, "Worshipping Illusions: An Interview with Marion Woodman," *Parabola*, Summer 1987, parabola.org/2019/04/13/worshipping-illusions-an-interview-with-marion-woodman/.
4   Glennon Doyle, *Untamed* (New York, NY: The Dial Press, 2020).
5   Roy T. Bennett, *The Light in the Heart: Inspirational Thoughts for Living Your Best Life* (Roy Bennett, 2016).

Chapter 10: Sovereign Love

Epigraph: James Hollis, *The Eden Project: In Search of the Magical Other* (Toronto, Canada: Inner City Books, 1998), 64.
1   Barbra Streisand, "Barbra Streisand—People," BarbraTV, August 1, 2012, YouTube video, 3:39, youtube.com/watch?v=fPlQ6EtArSc.
2   Iyanla Vanzant, "Iyanla Explains Why She Ended Her 14-Year Relationship | Iyanla: Fix My Life | Oprah Winfrey Network," OWN, October 28, 2017, YouTube video, 1:28, youtube.com/watch?v=q1-7P85kF6w.
3   "Ram Dass Quotes," Ram Dass Love Serve Remember Foundation, accessed September 9, 2023, ramdass.org/ram-dass-quotes/.
4   Marianne Williamson, *A Return to Love: Reflections on the Principles of A Course in Miracles* (New York: Harper Perennial, 1992).
5   Pablo Neruda, *100 Love Sonnets: Cien Sonetos de Amor* (Austin, TX: University of Texas Press, 2014).

About the Author

dené Logan is a marriage and family therapist, a group facilitator, a speaker, and an author based in Los Angeles. In addition to working with clients in private practice, she is a mindfulness coach, a yoga teacher, a tenacious wisdom seeker, and a California soul through and through. She is known for her nurturing presence and authenticity, as well as making spiritual principles tangible for utilizing within our day to day lives. In her work as a therapist, Dené specializes in supporting couples with finding deeper fulfillment in their relationships, and utilizing her background in depth psychology to explore how each of us can reclaim the aspects of our selves we've been societally conditioned to turn away from. She facilitates several group immersive experiences and retreats every year and is also co-host of the podcast *Cheaper Than Therapy*.

About Sounds True

Sounds True was founded in 1985 by Tami Simon with a clear mission: to disseminate spiritual wisdom. Since starting out as a project with one woman and her tape recorder, we have grown into a multimedia publishing company with a catalog of more than 3,000 titles by some of the leading teachers and visionaries of our time, and an ever-expanding family of beloved customers from across the world.

In more than three decades of evolution, Sounds True has maintained our focus on our overriding purpose and mission: to wake up the world. We offer books, audio programs, online learning experiences, and in-person events to support your personal growth and awakening, and to unlock our greatest human capacities to love and serve.

At SoundsTrue.com you'll find a wealth of resources to enrich your journey, including our weekly *Insights at the Edge* podcast, free downloads, and information about our nonprofit Sounds True Foundation, where we strive to remove financial barriers to the materials we publish through scholarships and donations worldwide.

To learn more, please visit SoundsTrue.com/freegifts or call us toll-free at 800.333.9185.

Together, we can wake up the world.